AUDACITY

THE COURAGE TO LET GO AND LEAP

Niki Brown

Books By Niki Brown

There Is More! 8 Steps to Embracing the Greater You
Audacity The Courage to Let Go and Leap!

ACKNOWLEDGMENTS

I want to thank God for giving me the grace to write a second book. Only He knows how much more I enjoy speaking than writing! To my husband, best friend, lover and champion: Harold, your love, support, consistency and calm is everything to me. I love you. Myka, thank you for sharing your dreams of how successful you thought my book would be! You inspire me. To all of my warrior friends who have faced insurmountable odds; watching your courage and bravery has taught me how to stare back at fear, plant my feet on the ground and leap into the impossible. Thank you!

CONTENTS

Acknowledgments vii

Introduction: Destiny Is A Decision xi

Part 1: Audacity To Be Flawed 1

Chapter 1   Unashamed 3

Chapter 2   I Am Enough 12

Part 2: Audacity To Show Up 19

Chapter 3   I'm Here—You're Welcome! 21

Chapter 4   You Belong In The Room 29

Part 3: Audacity To Believe 33

Chapter 5   Pessimist Within 35

Chapter 6   Faith In Reverse 43

Chapter 7   Raise Your Cup 48

Part 4: Audacity To Look Again 59

Chapter 8   The Power Of Perspective 61

Chapter 9   Destiny In The Details 69

Part 5: Audacity To Walk Away 81

Chapter 10 If It Ain't Broke, Break It 83

Chapter 11 Divorce Your Plans 92

Chapter 12 Letting Go 98

Chapter 13 Grace To Say Goodbye 109

Part 6: Audacity To Leap 119

Chapter 14 Lessons In Leadership 121

Chapter 15 The One Decision 144

Chapter 16 Answer The Call 154

Chapter 17 Your Time is Now 171

Notes 175

DESTINY IS A DECISION

*"There is only one decision that separates those
who achieve success and those who just dream."*
—*Oprah Winfrey*

I t was time. I had put it off long enough. With sweaty hands, I grabbed the pen and signed the contract to launch one of the largest business ventures in my life. At the time I was living on food stamps, close to broke, and it felt as if I was signing my entire life away. While I had accomplished many things, this by far was the most daring risk I had ever taken. What if I can't pay for it? What happens if no one supports me? I'm already in debt. What will people say? What qualifies me to do this? Maybe I should wait a couple of years until things calm down in my finances.

Up until this point, I prided myself on being an astute planner. I knew how to organize the steps to accomplish a goal. I had perfected the art of always having a plan A, B, and C. If neither of those worked, then D, E, and F were never far away.

But at that moment there was only plan A. If that didn't work, I was going to fail miserably and my family would suffer the loss. But no matter what I said to talk myself out of that moment, I had this undeniable, palpable sense that sitting in that management office was exactly where I was supposed to be and signing that contract was exactly what I was destined to do. This one decision caused my entire life to leap into an incredible season that is now changing the lives of women everywhere.

Sometimes the only thing standing between you and destiny is a decision. That's it. One unnerving, audacious, out-of-the-box step which can change the entire trajectory of your life.

Have you been there? Standing on the edge of your worst fear and possibly your greatest opportunity? You don't have the resources or experiences to take the next step and you're second-guessing whether you heard God's voice or your own. But somewhere a part of you is screaming, "Girl, you can do this—take the leap," while the other part is shouting in protest, "Are you crazy? What are you thinking?" You spend weeks agonizing over it. You call all your friends and spiritual counselors for their opinions and guidance only to come back to the same place where you started. Alone, carrying the burden of a decision that only you can make. A decision, which unlike others, has the potential to change…everything.

Your decisions determine your destiny. Your life right now is a product of a decision you made somewhere in your past. You might reject this idea because maybe, like me, you believed other people were responsible for where you ended up in life.

In my book There is More, 8 Steps to Discovering the Greater You, I talk about how I blamed everyone for why my life was mediocre. I spent years waiting for someone to open a door and give me the thumbs-up sign signifying I was good enough and qualified for the life I really wanted to live. No matter how desperately I searched for this person, he or she never arrived because he or she didn't exist. God revealed to me that greatness and success don't just happen; you have to create it. Moment by moment, step by step. Decision by decision.

Do you want the truth? Making a decision is not easy. In fact, it can be agonizing. I'm not talking about everyday decisions, such as what you will wear to work or eat for lunch. I mean those life-changing, fork-in-the-road, do-or-die decisions. Even as I write this book, I realize that I spent the last nine months trying to decide if I even wanted to write the book. In truth, I was nervous. Would people really buy a second book? Were they just being nice and supportive when I wrote the first one?

For nine months I became stalled on a road called "should I." It's where you question yourself on what you suspect is something you're being called to do. Should I really move forward with this new business? Should I get married now? Should I leave my job and venture into something new? What will people think? What steps should I take?

Sound familiar? I think we've all been stuck on the road of "should I," "what if," "maybe," and "let's wait and see." But at the end of that road you will find a town called "stagnant, mediocre and frustrated." In other words, this is what you will experience if you stand on the cliff of indecision too long.

You may be saying, "That's just not my makeup. I'm not daring. I didn't have the best upbringing. My parents were divorced. I was raised poor. I didn't do well in school." Yup, I used to recite that list too. But one day God challenged me with a question: "What's the difference between you and Oprah Winfrey, or even Bill Gates?" I replied, "Okay, God, really? How about: Rich. Smart. Talented. Good Connections. Lucky breaks." He said, "No, it's none of those things. It's not their talents, gifts, connections or being in the right place at the right time. You can have all of that and remain stuck. The difference between you and them? They had the audacity to make a decision." That's it. They took a crazy, insane step to do something daring at the risk of their reputation, resources, and safety, guided by the belief that it was destiny.

I grew up in a charismatic religion where the word "audacity" was never used in a positive way. It was more like, "She had the audacity to stand up and say that?" Or "I can't believe you have the audacity to even think that was okay!" My generation and culture were taught to put our heads down, be quiet, and follow the rules. The idea of asking for more than we deserved was seen as self-aggrandizing. Taking risks without a solid fall-back plan was foolish, and for heaven's sake don't even think about leaving your job if you don't have another one already. I'm convinced that a whole generation of gifted individuals are still living trapped in the mediocrity of the mundane. I adopted this mindset too and always wrestled with the unspoken question of "Who do you think you are?" whenever I attempted to do anything against the grain.

I had to do my own research on this word to understand why it created such a sense of contempt. What I learned is that audacity is a behavior that butts up against every rule and norm, so much so that it makes others feel uncomfortable. So here's my definition of it: audacity is an unrestricted boldness to do something that is outside and beyond your comfort zone. It is a courageous vulnerability to put yourself out there in spite of the possibility that it just might fail. Audacity is not born out of your skill, competency or ability to do something efficiently. It's you making a decision to take a risk that you're not qualified to take—nor are you certain of the outcome. It's confidence in the face of no confidence, and as Romans 4:18 alludes to, it's "hope against hope."

This is why I don't believe audacity is a feeling but rather a belief system. It's a belief that goes beyond what you think you can achieve and taps into a greater source and undeniable conviction that says, God loves me, God is for me, and He wants me to win.

To be clear, audacity does not guarantee success no matter what. It's a posture that stands on the idea that in the face of possible defeat, I will embrace the truth of who I am, who God is, and what I feel destined to do in this moment.

I had to ask myself, where have I exhibited this kind of audacity? How have I been brave? What risks have I really taken in my life? Where have I disregarded normal constraints, thrown caution to the wind and done something truly daring? While I'd definitely had some daring moments, such as speaking in front of a crowd of several thousand or having a very difficult conversation, those moments didn't feel intentional or purposefully courageous. I was either assigned to do those things or felt pressured to do so. The ability to be audacious begins with a decision. An intentional, thought-out choice to do something that goes against every fiber of your being and challenges you to your core. I realized that I had very few times where I made a conscious decision to be brave. It was easier to be unintentionally audacious and rely on others to push me so that if it didn't work out, it wasn't my fault.

When I signed the contract for my very first women's summit, I learned that God was calling me to be brave on purpose. But I had a problem with this. Why would God leave something so powerful as destiny in the hands of a decision I would or wouldn't make? Truthfully, it seems a little irresponsible on God's part. He's created this amazing plan for us which has the potential to change and impact people's lives. Why would it boil down to a decision? I don't know about you, but I've made a lot of dumb decisions, especially during an emotional crisis or circumstance in which I felt forced to make an unwise choice.

I found the answer in Romans 8:28, which says, "All things work together for the good of them that love the Lord and are called according to His purpose." God in His infinite wisdom and omniscience knew us before we were born. Jeremiah 1:5 says, "I chose you before I formed you in the womb; I set you apart before you were born." He not only formed me, but He intimately knows me and every single step that I will take. He knew the tears I would cry, the victories I would experience and the mistakes I would make. I'm a firm believer that God is not passive in His approach to my life in that He sits back and watches what I will do. I believe He works sovereignly behind the scenes to bring my life to the place that He purposed all along.

Therefore, God will never force me to make the right decisions, but He doesn't cancel out my future from a bad decision either. In God's grace and mercy for us, He ensures that even the negative decisions will be added in to work for our good. So no matter what detours your life has taken or mistakes you've made, Romans 8:28 tells me that you have the exact past God wants you to have and every step you take will work for your good in the end. In other words, where you are right now is exactly where God expected you to be.

If that's the case, why do you even need audacity? If God is going to fulfill His promise in your life anyway, why do you need courage? Why do you have to do things that are uncomfortable and scary? Truthfully, you don't. You can live passively and wait for things to happen. You can hope for a door to open in the areas you've been praying for or you can take steps that will manifest what's already waiting for you.

Audacity is a driving force that puts your faith into action and accelerates the results. Brene Brown wrote in Daring Greatly, "You can choose courage or you can choose comfort, but you cannot have both." You can't have both because courage creates movement in your life, while comfort creates mediocrity. Audacity breaks patterns. It demolishes routines. It moves the needle and forces a new normal to develop. I would dare say that audacity can expedite the accomplishment of your goals. What would've happened if I had risked writing this book nine months ago? I'm pretty certain I would be traveling on tour right now. Even though Romans 8:28 teaches us that in the end we will get to our destines, how quickly we get there is up to us.

So let me tell you what this book will do for you and what it won't:

This book will not be a pep talk on how to live your best life. Living with audacity means learning how to get in the ring with an opponent much bigger and stronger than you, whether that be your doubt, fear or inner critic. It's being willing to take some hits and even lose a few rounds, and then having the courage to get back in the ring and do it again. While that can lead to your best life, walking in courage is a journey—one that will require all your resolve, strength and faith.

This book will not help you overcome your fear. No, audacity finds out where fear lives and moves in with it. It's only when you look fear in the eyes that your courageous and daring self comes alive. It's when you stand toe to toe and wrestle with your greatest misgivings, insecurities, and shortcomings that you discover your power to win. I'm a big Marvel fan and realized that while each superhero had an amazing gift, it didn't start out that way. All of them were faced with their worst fears and crises, which stirred up their inner warriors. Your crisis is critical to your development. It's in your weakness that you will find your strength and courage.

Finally, this book will not be a step-by-step guide on how to obtain a quick miracle. While some courageous acts and prayer will produce overnight results, audacity is a lifestyle—one that starts in your mind, takes up residence in your heart and is manifested through your decisions.

What I pray this book will do is speak to your indecisions, whisper in the ear of inactivity, and challenge you to get up and face every excuse you've used to manage a life of mediocrity and hide behind a spiritual lingo that makes it okay to do nothing.

This book is to remind you of who you are as well as who God is and has been in your life. He has your best interest at heart and will never and has never let you fall. He has created you for more and truly wants you to have the more you crave.

Finally, my hope is that you will meet Him back at the place where you abandoned your dreams, ideas, gifts, and talents due to fear, rejection, or not being seen as good enough, and that you will finally embrace your God-given destiny to let go... and leap.

PART 1
AUDACITY TO BE FLAWED

CHAPTER 1

UNASHAMED

"It's not always your successes that make
you beautiful..but your scars."
—*Niki Brown*

"No, I just can't...do it." I pushed my worksheet aside, put my head down on the desk and cried. My second-grade teacher shook her head in disgust and muttered (for all my classmates to hear), "It's a shame you're such a crybaby." The pain and embarrassment I experienced in that moment spoke louder than her words. I decided right then I would never let anyone see me as weak, small, or vulnerable again. It started a lifelong journey of living under the motto "I'm gonna fake it till I make it."

For years, I did a good job of staying committed to it. From the outside I appeared strong, independent and unbreakable. I built up a solid fortress that kept those "weak emotions" like fear, vulnerability, guilt, hurt and affection from rearing its ugly head in my relationships. I prided myself on not being "weak" and looked down my nose at other women who fell apart at struggle, cried at commercials, or simply didn't "have it together" like they should. I made sure that each time I left the house my hair, nails and appearance were together, and whenever I entered a room I put up a facade that said "don't mess with me." I fought back at any criticism I received with well-crafted excuses that shifted the blame onto anyone…but me. From the outside I appeared fearless, bold and strong.

I was an impostor.

Or as my teenage daughter would say, I was "being fake." The courage to be authentic died the day I was chastised for being vulnerable. It took close to twenty years to resurrect that little girl and convince her it was okay to simply be…herself.

Audacity begins with authenticity. I don't believe you can have one without the other. True authenticity is having the courage to show up and live in a way that's in harmony with what you believe, feel, and think. It's having the intentional boldness to fight back or walk away from anything that is not in alignment with your core values, desires, or purpose. I spent most of my life running away from this type of audacity. It was scary and uncomfortable. Plus, it required a naked vulnerability that put me at risk of being rejected or ridiculed. So I pretended that I was strong and bold. I put on a facade of fearlessness. The only problem was in order to accomplish my dreams I needed to *be* authentically bold. I needed to step out of my comfort zone and make intentional decisions that could possibly damage my "perfect" image if things didn't work out.

Have you ever faced this dilemma? Where you're stuck between exhibiting true courage and maintaining the facade of one? Social media has made it easy to craft an image that we want the world to see. Many of us do our best to live up to that image. Somewhere along the way real-life pain and heartbreak crack our facade, forcing us to face the truth and reality of who we really are.

Impostor Syndrome

I remember having this obsession to become someone else. I'm pretty certain it was not a conscious effort at the time, but it was real nonetheless. My entire life became centered around presenting a perfect image, one free from blemishes and any embarrassing or less than desirable traits. I created a shield to hide not only my emotions but also my intelligence, gifting, quirkiness, sensitivity, ideas and opinions. I acted this out by becoming a chameleon of sorts. I blended in. I did whatever was necessary to acquiesce to the prevailing thoughts, ideas, and conversations around me, even if it was to my detriment. If someone didn't like my hair, I changed it. If I was criticized for talking too loud, I quieted myself.

I worked hard to fold myself into whatever shape necessary to get acceptance and approval. The benefit—or so I thought—was that I avoided conflict. I did everything I could to be likable and agreeable. If I happened to get involved in any dispute, I quickly worked to bring resolution so I could be likable again.

The downside of pretending was that I was unable to take ownership of the successes I actually did achieve. I disregarded praise or compliments and saw them as illegitimate. I lived with the fear that any day someone would figure out that I was a fake and a fraud. It's called "The Impostor Syndrome," which is the persistent belief and fear that all your gifts, talents, and accomplishments are invalid and that eventually you'll be seen as a fraud. You believe that you're not what people think and you don't deserve the acknowledgment you've received because somehow you didn't earn it—you just got lucky.

The Impostor Syndrome is a messy cycle. It works like this: Let's say you've been given an assignment to complete, whether at work or school or in ministry. You feel anxious or nervous about completing the assignment because you question your ability to do it. If you're like me, you may procrastinate or over-prepare. If you procrastinate, you will rush to get it finished, stressing yourself and everyone else around you. Once you've finished and if you receive positive feedback, you temporarily feel good but eventually will discount your accomplishment because you believe you pulled a rabbit out of your hat.

If you're the type that over-prepares, you will be plagued with self-doubt and second-guess each decision and step you take. The process to complete the task is agonizingly longer than it should be. If you receive positive feedback, you will only see it as a result of hard work and not give credit for personal ability or gifting. Because of how much hard work you had to endure and how long the process took, you may dread facing the next assignment.

And the cycle just continues.

In the end, no matter how much praise or how many accolades you receive, it's not enough to convince you that you're the "real deal." In spite of everything you've done and accomplished, there is a voice that says, "It's not enough, and you are not enough." So you push yourself to work harder or hide behind procrastination and excuses to prevent people from finding out who you really are.

Sound familiar? While you might not fit that example perfectly, if you've experienced these feelings, you're probably struggling through this syndrome. You are not alone. Studies suggest that nearly seventy percent of individuals will experience signs and symptoms of impostor phenomenon at least once in their lives.

Setting Yourself Free

To be truly authentic, I had to confront the one stumbling block that kept me from being real: shame. Shame is the pain you experience when you believe or perceive that others see you as inferior or unworthy of love because of something you've done, thought, or experienced. Shame teaches you that a part of who you are and how you feel must be silenced, hidden, and closed off for fear of rejection, ridicule and abandonment.

Shame attaches itself to your experience and identity. So if you were abused, shame tells you that you are unlovable. If you experienced being molested, shame will whisper that you are dirty. When I was scolded for crying in second grade, shame told me I was weak and incapable of success. If you made mistakes, shame makes you believe that you are a mistake.

The natural tendency then is to hide those parts of yourself that you believe will be viewed as lacking, unlovable, or inadequate. So shame acts like an anchor. No matter how desperately you want to be authentic, shame keeps the real you hidden and grounded. The desire to hide and put up a cover feels necessary to survive. The experience in my second-grade class led me to hide my emotions and feelings for fear of being labeled as weak. It makes it understandable why sexual abuse survivors stay quiet for years and sometimes never share their experiences. The survivors I have counseled struggled more with discussing the feelings of shame versus the abuse itself.

One of the greatest tools you can use to become free of shame is changing your perspective of the past. We've all experienced something in our lives that's been painful and at times debilitating, but the greater challenge is not what happened to us, but what we tell ourselves about it. Shame is born because of how we interpret the events of our past. More specifically, it's the labels we create and attach to our identity.

For example, if your father was absent from your life as a child, you may have decided that something was wrong with you to cause your father to not be present. The idea that your own parent doesn't want to be connected to you brings an incredible sense of shame. You silently label yourself as unlovable. Your greatest fear is opening yourself to that hurt again, so you create a persona or an image that you hope prevents others from abandoning you. You may struggle with the feelings of being an impostor when someone truly expresses love and wants to be in a relationship.

But if you were to change your perspective you might see your father's absence had nothing to do with you. It's possible your father didn't have the capacity to be who you needed. He should've had the capacity, but he didn't. You are not responsible for who your father chose to be. I like to believe that in God's sovereign plan for your life, He understood that your father being absent may have benefitted you more than his presence. Changing your perspective will help you create a different conclusion. Instead of believing you were being rejected—maybe you were being rescued.

The good news is we no longer have to carry the shame of our past. When Jesus died on the cross, He decided to take ownership of and carry away all of our guilt, sin and pain. Romans 8:1 teachers us, "There is therefore now no condemnation(shame) to those who are in Christ Jesus, who do not walk after the flesh but according to the Spirit." Jesus didn't want the labels, lies, pain, abuse and mistakes of our past to haunt us and remain attached to our identity. He wanted us to live unashamed. Jesus's death on the cross made a way for us to exchange our old identity for a new one. Our new identity is not rooted in fear or pain, but in Christ's love, righteousness, power and His ultimate purpose and plan for us.

Speak Your Way Out

When I was working through my graduate counseling program, my classmates and I were informed that we would be required to go through group counseling sessions. The professors believed that "you can't take a person to a place you have never been." I really struggled the first six months with group counseling because I didn't want to speak about the shame of my childhood. I had been molested by an older family friend and was teased and degraded daily for being dark-skinned and skinny. As a child, I never felt that I measured up to the other kids in my neighborhood. I was very much ashamed of these experiences, and speaking about them felt like death to me. I feared the negative perceptions I had about myself would become real the more I spoke about my experiences.

True to form I approached the request to be vulnerable with resistance and tried to convey to my group that I had nothing to discuss in my past. For weeks I sat in silence, listening in judgment as I watched others cry and talk about their pasts. One day my professor took me to the side and challenged me, saying, "You don't seem to be open to this process."

I told her, "I am open. I'm just not crying over my past as it's over."

She lovingly but sternly told me that I was being self-righteous and maybe God was trying to do something new in my life. While I was offended, I knew she was right. I was terrified of opening a Pandora's box of my past pain. But I decided that I was in this program for a reason and finally began to share. Something interesting and unexpected happened. The more I spoke about my pain, the less potent and god-like it was. Instead of feeling horrible or experiencing the judgment I thought others would give, I felt as if a fifty-pound weight had been lifted off me.

Sometimes we exalt the pain of our pasts and place it on a pedestal or shrine to worship. Don't worry, I'm not accusing you of paganism, but I want you to see this analogy: the pain of our pasts becomes a demigod. It dictates everything—our relationships, our responses, and our ability to reach for new goals and dreams. When the past is not confronted, it sits on the altar and demands we sacrifice our lives to it. While we don't do this consciously, subconsciously and spiritually we do. But like all false gods in the Bible, eventually they must be confronted and torn down. Brene Brown, author of Daring Greatly, reveals the cure for overcoming shame. She says, "Shame cannot survive being spoken. It cannot survive empathy." Shame sits on the altar of silence, but it dies when it's given sound. Shame has to be spoken to for its power to be broken.

Your story and your voice become weapons to disarm the power of shame. You may have to do it in a safe environment like counseling or with a group of loved ones you trust. Either way, speaking about the shame breaks its power and hold over you. Not only that, but empathy and love must be extended in the place where you judged yourself unworthy and unlovable. To become free, you will need to speak to the parts of yourself hiding in shame and say, "You may have made some mistakes, but you are not a mistake. You went through it, but you are not it."

CHAPTER 2

I AM ENOUGH

*"You alone are enough. You have
nothing to prove to anybody."*
—*Maya Angelou*

The Imposter Syndrome always leads to the pressure to prove. As I travel to various conferences and seminars to speak, I often encounter women who have the same look: hungry for more yet drained and exhausted from doing. A good friend of mine likes to use the phrase "I have my 'S' on my chest today." She is referring to the superwoman phenom. It's the need some women feel to keep it all together and prove that they're strong at all times. The expectation to be everything to everybody without fail is one of the most common complaints I've heard from women in my counseling practice.

I've found that the more gifted you are, the more pressure there is to please people and prove your worth. You've probably figured out that competency is only rewarded with more demands to produce. You may have initially enjoyed the feeling of being needed and the compliments on how awesome you were. But eventually the weekly requests from family, friends, ministry leaders, and coworkers to be at their beck and call become overwhelming, frustrating and downright exhausting. You don't feel courageous enough to tell people no because if you do, they might perceive that you're really not competent after all. Maybe they will see that you're not selfless or the superwoman you claim to be. So to prove yourself, you keep nodding your head yes and going along to get along because the fear of not living up to people's expectations is worse than your need for rest and the ability to reclaim your time.

If this sounds familiar it's because somewhere in your life you bought into the myth and lie that you are not enough. So you've been working to be more, do more and prove to the people around you that you are "that girl." Superwoman. Indestructible. Invaluable. Significant. Worthy. You can handle anything—anytime, anywhere. Bring it on. But that's only during the day when everyone is watching. When you're alone, you're anxious, afraid, frustrated, maybe depressed and definitely exhausted.

Sometimes the pressure comes from external forces, such as our families, friends and spouses. But more often the pressure comes from within. My second-grade teacher passed away years after that incident, but that didn't stop me from trying to prove to her that I was not weak or a crybaby. I found myself working hard at preventing emotions like fear or hurt from rising to the surface in my relationships. While many of those who criticized my weight, hair and skin complexion were no longer alive or in my life, I did everything I could to internally prove that I was in fact beautiful and deserving of love and respect.

So here's a question for you: are you living for ghosts? Are you trying to prove to individuals who are gone from your life that you're good enough? Jesus was often under pressure to prove who He was too. All throughout the Gospels, it was recorded how the Pharisees and Sadducees (Jewish Leaders) put Jesus under a microscope and critiqued and criticized everything He did. The crowds followed Him everywhere, wanting Him to literally produce a miracle. Everyone was desperate to know if He was legitimate and the long-awaited Messiah.

John 10:24 shows us one of these instances: "These leaders gathered around Jesus, asking, 'How long will you keep us in suspense? If you are the Messiah, tell us plainly.' Jesus answered, 'I did tell you, but you do not believe. The works I do in my Father's name testify about me.'" Even when they rejected Him as the Messiah, Jesus never doubted who He was. He didn't stop working on what He was sent to earth to do. Despite the pressure to work miracles and provide signs for the people, Jesus was content in knowing His works had already spoken for Him. He didn't need the validation or approval of anyone to confirm it.

You have to be careful that you don't become so emotionally connected to what "they" think or so focused on trying to prove yourself whether on social media, in church or on your job that you lack the clarity you need to fulfill your destiny. Sometimes you have to pause and ask yourself, "Why am

I doing this? Am I doing it for the applause and approval of people? Or is there something authentic in me that's doing it because it's who I am?"

During my counseling program one of my professors said, "Niki, when your goal is to appease people, you will struggle under the weight and pressure to produce and perform. You will overexert yourself to prove your value just to end up at the same place you started: frustrated, exhausted, and rejected. But when you authentically know who you are and who God has created you to be, you don't have to prove yourself to anyone. You can just be."

The Problem is the Solution

That's it? Just be? I wasn't crazy about the idea of just letting go and being myself. What if no one likes how I "be?"

"What if I'm not enough?"

My professor responded by saying, "Niki, those who were meant to embrace you will. Those who were not—won't."

That simple response changed my life. This had to be the perspective that Jesus used which enabled Him to be unbothered by the demands, the pressures of the people and the temptation to prove Himself. In John 6:64-65, He said, "'But there are some of you who do not believe.' For Jesus knew from the beginning who they were who did not believe, and who would betray Him. And He said, 'Therefore I have said to you that no one can come to Me unless it has been granted to him by My Father.'" If the Savior of the entire world knew that He wasn't going to save everyone nor prove to all that He was the Messiah, how much more can we do in trying to prove ourselves?

This was my "aha" moment. The solution to being free of the suffocating feelings of shame was not to run away from who I was—or try and prove that I was better than my past. The solution was for me to embrace my past. To become intimately acquainted with the broken parts of myself that I so desperately wanted to hide. And instead of hating myself for what I saw as blemishes, inadequacies and embarrassing experiences in my life, I needed to actually accept that those were the exact things that made me great.

In order to be free, I had to be me. The problem was the solution. How many years had I wasted trying to validate something about myself that was already real and true? I was beautiful, different, unique and sensitive. I was powerful, resilient, creative and strong. But I was also selfish at times, moody, picky and self-righteous. I made mistakes—lots of them—and had a difficult past.

But that was me. All of it—the good, the bad and the ugly.

Authenticity is not just knowing your truth—it's being able to embrace it too. It's being willing to own your strengths, weaknesses, idiosyncrasies, successes, failures, shortcomings, past mistakes, gifts, talents and abilities. To not downplay a promotion or an award, believing you don't deserve it. Nor is it downgrading yourself because you're not who people want you to be. It's owning your status in life even if what you do seems small and insignificant.

Authenticity is having the audacity to just be. It's having the courage to say to yourself, I am enough. There is nothing missing or lacking in you. It's being able to accept that the people who love and support you don't need you to prove anything. They love you because of what they see in you. You are enough. You've always been enough.

Finally, being authentic requires having the courage to look your past in the eye and declare that the abuse, trauma, and pain were not a mistake. You...are not a mistake. Everything you experienced was purposeful, intentional and allowed by an all-knowing, all-seeing God to the end that you would be exactly who He wanted you to be.

Broken yet blessed.

Flawed and favored.

PART 2
AUDACITY TO
SHOW UP

CHAPTER 3

I'M HERE—YOU'RE WELCOME!

Our greatest fear is not that we are inadequate,
but that we are powerful beyond measure. It is
our light, not our darkness, that frightens us.
—*Marianne Williamson*

Have you ever noticed how some people can walk into a room as if they own it without saying a word? They just seem to have the "it" factor. From their hair and clothes to their poise and energy, they seem to be saying, "I'm here, you're welcome!" You don't know whether to love or hate them because while you may be offended, you're impressed at the same time. If you pay close attention, you will discover that their intrigue is not solely based on their physical appearance or their ability to speak and engage others in an impactful way.

They have something more: presence.

We all have it. It's how people experience you and the energy you exude when you connect and engage with others, whether at work, church or home. While we all have presence, most of us are not aware of the type of presence we carry. As a public speaker and leader, I didn't understand how important presence was. During my early years of speaking, I didn't pay attention to how I came across to others. Most of the time I was so nervous and worried about messing up that I just wanted to finish my presentation and sit down. I started to notice, however, that I wasn't receiving callbacks to speak in places where I visited.

Additionally, while the teams I was leading were very productive, I was not being invited to the cookouts and the baby showers. For a while I pretended it didn't bother me. But I believe God used these moments as a wake-up call to gently nudge me into transforming some aspects of my life.

One day, while in a conversation with one of my leaders, he said, "Niki, you are gifted and talented. But some people think that you're mean and unapproachable. You walk in a room and don't say hello, you rarely smile, and you don't engage in conversations with anyone."

I was completely floored. Me? "I'm the nicest person you want to know!"

He said, "Yes, I know that—but that's not how you show up."

I walked away confused, angry and honestly a little offended. I went home and rationalized why people would think this about me. Of course, my rationale at the time was a little self-righteous. I remember thinking, Some people are just so sensitive! I'm here to get a job done and not babysit anyone's feelings! If people got to know me, they would see how nice I am. But I am not going to chase anybody. I am who I am, and they need to either accept me or not.

I didn't know that my struggle to be vulnerable and let my guard down around people created an image that appeared closed, unengaged and unapproachable. While this wasn't my intention, the impact was undeniable.

Impact vs. Intent

There are times when who you are and how you show up are at odds with one another. In private there is a you that is completely different than the you that shows up in the world. You may have spent so many years crafting an image that works in public that you're not aware your public image is incongruent with your private persona. When you're unaware of how you show up, your intent and impact start working against each other. For example, you may not intend for people to perceive you as shy or aggressive, but you've been hearing from others that they identify you as such. It's frustrating because you can't figure out the disconnect or what you are doing to give people this impression.

Let me give you another example. If you lead teams of people, you may have a desire to be seen as a leader who is strong, secure and competent. You want people to see you as approachable and willing to help others succeed. But based on the feedback you've received, this intention is not coming through. Instead, you've been accused of being bossy, aggressive, pushy, demanding at times, and aloof.

These examples may not fit you perfectly, but I'm sure you would agree that there have been times when your intention and your impact were not in line, whether it was communicating something that was received the wrong way or actions you took which didn't have the desired results. Or maybe it's just your personality and how it comes across to others. Somewhere along the way, who you are and how you presented yourself were out of touch.

Now, you're probably asking the question, "What type of presence should I have then?" Is it realistic that I show up smiling all the time when I don't feel like it? Should I pretend to be happy or loving of others when that's not my personality? The answer is no. Having presence is not coming into a room and putting on a show to make people believe that you're one thing when you are not. It's not "faking it till you make it." Presence is the ability to show up in a way where who you really are and who you want to be is on full display.

When You Show Up

After weeks of sulking over the comments from my leader and others, I accepted the truth. I was not showing up in a way that was consistent with who I was and wanted to be. I did walk past people without speaking. I intentionally looked very serious or pissed off when I entered a room. I had perfected the 'I don't really care' face. Even more so, I didn't engage myself to get to know others around me or those whom I led. But I knew I was a sensitive, caring, funny and charismatic person.

I also wanted to be approachable and open as a leader and friend. But I was more worried about being seen as vulnerable and weak. My greater anxiety was that I would become that eight-year-old in the second grade who was admonished and rejected for showing her emotions, or that ten-year-old being teased on the playground. Worse, I feared being seen as insignificant and small.

To counteract those fears, I created a hard-nosed, "don't mess with me" image which I thought would protect me from being hurt and rejected. Ironically these self-protective measures created the very response that I feared. I was rejected even more and misperceived. As much as I wanted to positively impact those around me, I carried a presence that betrayed my deepest desire to be real, authentic and confident.

Who are you really in public? Do you diminish your personality to make others more comfortable around you? Or do you put up a self-protective wall to prevent people from knowing the real you? Do you work to be the center of attention for fear of being ignored or viewed as insignificant?

More importantly how do you show up in life? I've noticed that as women with busy schedules and "to do" lists, we rush through life versus living it. Life is happening to us. Which means you are surviving day to day rather than crafting the life you were destined for. God doesn't want you to just survive. He built you to show up and live. At times showing up means having a determination to face your problems and not run from them. Or it's choosing to be consistent in your efforts to grow at work and in your relationships. It's pushing past obstacles and being present in the moment no matter how difficult that moment might be. Either way showing up is having the courage to bring your most authentic self to every step you take, goal you attempt to fulfill, and obstacle you encounter.

It took me a while to acknowledge that I wanted to show up differently. There were areas in my life where I was not present and needed to be more accountable. I had spent most of my life hiding and blaming everything and everyone for my struggles and failures. I needed to take control of things that I had he power to change and not allow life to just happen. What I really wanted was to carry a presence that felt warm, inviting and authentic to others. I wanted others to feel accepted around me yet also challenged and inspired. Furthermore, I desired to overcome the feelings of intimidation, insecurity and unworthiness when I was faced with situations that were bigger than my experience and threatened to expose my inadequacies.

My passion to touch others and be an authentic leader, mother, wife, friend, neighbor and minister started to grow more important than my need for self-protection. So little by little I took courageous steps to initiate connection, open my soul, and be vulnerable and authentic with the men and women around me. It took lots of prayer and courage to let those walls down and allow people into my heart and life, but the results were noticeable. People, especially women, started to seek out my company, not always to talk, but just to be in my presence.

Power in Your Presence

The real work was fighting to change the negative perception I had of myself which created those self-protective walls in the first place. It was during this process that I discovered something important. Presence is built on perspective—not just the perspective of yourself, but also your perspective of how you think others perceive you. I honestly believed that if I allowed others close to me, they would see me as insignificant, small and weak. None of these things were true, but I built a presence based off that perspective anyway.

You will show up looking like what you believe. Until you change your perspective and abandon the lies you've endorsed, you will create an image that's right in line with your belief system. If you believe that who you are and what you have is unimportant, you will show up and blend into the walls and background. If you believe that you must be seen and heard, you will overcompensate to be the center of attention. If you were told that you are too loud and direct, you will diminish your voice and ideas. If you don't really know who you are, you will show up trying to be everything for everybody.

Now, I hear some of you arguing with me and wondering, "Why do I need presence? I'm good. I don't need to enter a room and be the center of attention. Nor do I feel the need to be an open book. I already have a solid set of friends who know who I am. Isn't that enough?"

Yes, it could be enough. But not if you want more. Not if you want to impact the people in your world more. Not if you've been called to lead, connect, or reach others beyond your circle of close friends. You can definitely be safe and live on the fringes of life. But you will be settling. And truthfully being safe will never satisfy the deep longing you have to make an impact and difference in your world.

You may have a hard time believing this, but your presence is needed. It's needed in your family, community, church, board room, job, neighborhood and maybe around the world. God has placed something unique within you that was meant to be shared with others. Someone needs your humor, kindness, creativity, vision, insight, gifting, quirkiness, sensitivity, talent and ability.

Your presence has the power to change someone's entire life. Jesus understood the power of His presence. Luke 5:21 says, "And it came to pass on a certain day, as He was teaching, that there were Pharisees and doctors of the law sitting by, who had come from every town of Galilee and Judea and Jerusalem. And the power of the Lord was present to heal them."

You don't have to be a miracle worker like Jesus to have power in your presence. When you show up with an openness and vulnerability to allow your gifts and personality to be on display, the power to heal, encourage, comfort or help will be experienced by all. Your presence is not about being popular. It's about owning the truth of who you are and letting the entire world in on that secret.

CHAPTER 4

YOU BELONG IN THE ROOM

*"To live an audacious life you have to get
to worthy. It's where you walk in the room
and say I'm supposed to be here."*
—Tyler Perry

What I didn't know was that God was cultivating my presence because He had plans for me to enter rooms with individuals who would greatly impact my destiny. These rooms were relationships—connections with individuals who stood taller than I did in terms of experience, education, talent and ability. Not only was God preparing me for relationships, but He also had plans for me to enter physical rooms where I would be given opportunities to stand before individuals of high prominence to utilize my gift and talent.

A few years ago, I had the opportunity to be a keynote speaker at a conference with hundreds of entrepreneurs, CEOs, industry leaders and influencers around that region. It was a fairly large event. To say I was nervous was an understatement. My comfort zone at that time revolved around speaking at smaller church functions.

For weeks I fought against anxiety and panic. What if I don't do well? I'm the keynote speaker, for goodness' sake! There are no other options for the attendees if my session doesn't go well. What do I really know about running a business anyway? Lord, why did I agree to this? The more I ruminated on my fears, the more anxious I became, and after weeks of driving myself into mental and emotional exhaustion, I felt the presence of God saying, "Niki, you belong in the room."

Getting To Worthy

That one statement spoke to an unspoken fear that I had harbored most of my life: Do I really belong here? Am I worthy? Surprisingly, with all my degrees and experience in counseling, I didn't know I'd been carrying around the question of my worth. I probably hid these feelings behind a sense of false humility. This is when someone comes across with what appears to be a wonderful attitude of servitude, but deep down she's only serving because she doesn't feel worthy enough to be served.

The danger in feeling unworthy is it convinces you to disown the opportunities God extends to you. I can think back to moments when I walked into certain doors carrying an air of apology for being present, meaning I folded myself to become invisible or less threatening to offend anyone. I would downsize my gift and talent because I felt guilty for being chosen for the opportunity. Worse, I remember the doors and opportunities

I never walked through because I was convinced my presence wasn't good enough.

Don't misunderstand. None of us are worthy. None of us deserve what we have because we're so good, talented or smart. Rather, God is good and extends to us that goodness in a way that we cannot buy, earn or repay. His only requirement is that we receive it and own it. In Tyler Perry's book Higher is Waiting, he discusses the struggle he experienced with feelings of unworthiness: "To live an audacious life you have to get to worthy. It's where you walk in the room and say I'm supposed to be here."

During my presentation, I had to tap into a courage that went beyond my natural confidence to speak. I already knew I was a good speaker. I didn't need tutoring on how to develop my presentation. What I needed was the audacity to believe "I'm supposed to be here, and I am enough." I have enough to walk in this room and any other room with an air of unapologetic, authentic confidence that says "I am here—you are welcome!"

I believe you're reading this right now because God is calling you to be a risk-taker. He is inviting you to enter rooms that are above your experience, education, status and comfort zone. Audacity is not the ability to enter a room because you have it all together. Audacity is the ability to identify how you stand out in that room. Audacity is you entering those rooms not knowing if you will qualify or be accepted or even found to be worthy. It's having the courage to believe "I belong here anyway!"

PART 3
AUDACITY TO BELIEVE

CHAPTER 5
PESSIMIST WITHIN

*"Real courage is seeing the glass as half full with
faith to believe the other half is on the way."*
—Niki Brown

I think I was born a pessimist. I'm embarrassed to admit this, but it's true. As early as I can remember I'd always feared and believed the worst. I can't point my finger to where or how I became pessimistic; I'd always been that way. As a child, I didn't have a definition or word for this consistent feeling of dread that the worst was going to happen at any minute. But I carried that feeling everywhere. It affected everything, from my grades, to making new friends in school, to deciding if I was going to try out for certain opportunities, and the list goes on.

It wasn't until years later when my husband, Harold, was trying to convince me that building our first home would be a good idea that he put a label on my lifelong doubt. He said, "Niki, you're such a pessimist." I quickly responded (and told him what most pessimists say when confronted with their own truth), "I am not a pessimist; I am a realist!" Something in that exchange, however, made me reflect on it and ask, "Am I really a pessimist?" Still in denial I looked up the definition, which read, "a tendency to see the worst aspect of things or believe that the worst will happen." Webster goes on to describe it this way: "Pessimism is a mental attitude in which an undesirable outcome is anticipated from a given situation. Pessimists tend to focus on the negatives of life in general. A common question asked to test for pessimism is 'Is the glass half empty or half full?'; in this situation a pessimist is said to see the glass as half empty, while an optimist is said to see the glass as half full."

Yup—that was me. The only thing missing was my picture posted next to the definition. It was hard to believe that despite my theological training, years of teaching the gospel, studies on faith, and prayer life, I carried around this cynical outlook and frail belief system. But it was true. The majority of my thoughts and feelings were somewhat negative and critical.

Maybe you weren't born a pessimist—if that's even possible—but you've had circumstances and events to change your perspective and influence your perception of life's possibilities. It may not have happened all at once. But slowly through time and disappointment, you carry around a feeling or belief that what you hope for will not happen. Even more so, you anticipate that around each corner something bad is waiting to destroy you, your dreams or the people you love. When you're a pessimist, having high expectations feels foolish and dangerous. The disappointments in life have taught you that you probably won't get what you want, so don't bother praying for it. You experienced so much, adversity, loss, frustration and struggle that to hope and believe seems more like a burden than a blessing.

If you're like me, you've learned to hide your pessimism behind the veil of Christian maturity and a spiritual lingo that makes it okay to downsize your hope and anticipation. This was evident in my prayers, which sounded like this: "God, I really wish You would bless me with a new car, but I am not sure You will, and if You don't, I will be satisfied..." Or "God, if You don't do another thing, I am grateful." What I was really saying was, "God, I believe You can do it; I just don't expect You to do it for me."

Right now, you may be having an argument in your mind that sounds something like this: "Look, Niki, I get that I am supposed to believe that all things are possible, but I'm just a realist and the facts are the facts. Why believe and hope for things that are completely out of my reach?" But a pessimist and realist are not the same thing. A realist sees both the good and bad in the world and proceeds based on the facts. A pessimist sees only the negative aspects of the world and uses that information as a reason to not take a step of faith. Instead, she puts God in a box because things don't make sense.

Faith Over Facts

The bigger problem in the logic of the pessimist and realist is they both discount faith. The pessimist believes that if she can't see it, then it's not real. The realist needs to rely on facts to make her next step. But walking in faith is not contingent on what you can see or having a good understanding of the facts. Faith is an inner conviction and belief with no physical evidence. And the things you believe by faith are not often supported by the facts. The truth is you don't need to exercise faith for things you can see and achieve on your own. Faith is needed for the things you can't see. Faith is needed for the circumstances and dreams that seem absolutely impossible. This type of faith is bold and courageous because it's not based on your skills or ability; it's based on you believing in God's power and grace to fulfill His promise and your heart's desires.

It takes audacity to believe. It takes audacity to believe in something that is beyond your paycheck, educational degree, and voice of doubt that tells you it won't happen. Your future follows your faith. You will never rise any higher than your faith system will allow. Proverbs 4:23 says, "Be careful how you think; your life is shaped by your thoughts" (GNT). Hebrews 11:6 says, "For without faith, it is impossible to please God, for he who comes to God must believe that He is and that He is a rewarder of those who diligently seek Him."

Faith is a divine confidence of things that have not been realized but are actively being expected. Everything flows from your faith. Your ability to achieve anything begins with faith. Every decision, step, and goal begins with your ability to believe beyond the moment you are in. There are moments when it's hard to embrace faith and have confidence in your future, especially when things look hopeless and you've experienced disappointments, hurt, and failure. But this is where the courage to believe is born. Audacious faith connects your trust with your courage. I like to believe that faith is the ship and audacity is the current that moves it.

Pessimism blocks your faith from being able to embrace the impossible. Even more so, pessimism shrinks your expectation to receive. I'm a firm believer that you prepare for what you expect. For instance, if you expect to wake up in the morning, you will most likely plan out your day. You will develop a schedule, perhaps, talk to others about what tomorrow is going to bring and prepare accordingly. But when you lack expectancy, your capacity to prepare for what's coming diminishes. The pessimist creates her own reality in that since she doesn't believe anything bigger is coming, she therefore doesn't plan for it. Because there is no plan, there is virtually no capacity for her to receive anything beyond her experience.

The Power to Believe

There are so many men and women in the Bible who walked with audacious faith. My favorite is a man named Abraham. In Genesis 12, Abraham was given a promise by God that he would have a son. Seems simple enough, right? But this promise involved more than just producing a natural heir. God also promised that this heir would produce more descendants than Abraham could count. He would bless Abraham and make him a blessing.

It was a promise of generational continuity, land abundance and prosperity. There was just one problem—Sarah,

Abraham's wife, could not have children. The Bible uses the term "barren." Sara couldn't call up her local doctor for a diagnosis or medicine to cure her. There were no medical opportunities for them to conceive artificially. No matter how often they tried, the results were always the same. Year after year she failed to produce this promise that God had given to them.

There is nothing more frustrating than being in a season that's contradictory to where you expected to prosper. Have you been there? You thought your life was headed in one direction, a positive direction, and all of a sudden you hit a wall. No matter what you tried to do, you couldn't seem to get past the block. What's frustrating about these seasons is the feeling of moving backward instead of moving into what you had believed for. God allowed Abraham to live in a contradiction for over thirty years. He had the power and means to produce a child but couldn't. Imagine waiting until you were nearly 100 years old to produce something that should have been within your power to accomplish years before.

What happened to Abraham's faith in the delay? Here's what the Bible says about it: "He considered his own body to be already dead (since he was about 100 years old) and also considered the deadness of Sarah's womb, without weakening in the faith. He did not waver in unbelief at God's promise but was strengthened in his faith and gave glory to God because he was fully convinced that what He had promised He was also able to perform." Abraham had the audacity to believe God's promise past the failure of his own physical body. Year after year while his physical ability diminished, his faith continued to grow. Because he had the courage to keep believing, the Bible says he was rewarded for his faith.

Sometimes your greatest destiny decision comes down to one daring act of simply believing. It sounds so simple, yet at the core of our spiritual walks, having the audacity to believe can be our greatest challenge. I've found it to be a lot easier to believe in certain things that are possible because you can predict the outcome and determine the steps. It's even easy to believe in the impossible for someone else. But do you have the audacity to *believe* the impossible for you? I'm not talking about asking for the impossible. We discuss this later in the book. But can you simply believe—for you?

How about when the math doesn't add up? Or when you lack adequate resources and support? Do you have the boldness to believe despite past disappointments, rejection, and people who may whisper "it won't work"? Can you summon the audacity to believe you can still have a baby or get married, or that God can heal your body and restore your kids when things look hopeless and too much time has passed?

God wants you to have that kind of audacity. It's this kind of audacity that led Mary, the mother of Jesus, to believe that she would conceive a child in spite of being a virgin. Not only did she believe she could conceive a child, but she believed the child would be the Messiah of the entire world.

Moses had the audacity to believe that despite being adopted and a convicted murderer, God had called him to deliver and lead over one million people out of Egypt and into their promise.

Sarah had the audacity to believe that she could give birth at ninety years old. There is a Hall of Fame of faith heroes listed in Hebrews chapter 11. They all used their faith to push themselves forward. Their life stories and circumstances could have given each of them the right to become doubtful, bitter and lose hope. But they didn't. They had audacity and denied pessimism the opportunity to rob them of their faith to believe God for the impossible despite overwhelming odds. Sometimes the next best step in your audacity journey is not what you should do but what you need to believe.

CHAPTER 6

FAITH IN REVERSE

"Don't fear opposition. Expect it. And use it
as an opportunity to fuel your growth."
—Steven Furtick

Audacious faith is having the ability to not only believe God for the incredible but also ask Him for it as well. I believe our prayer requests are in line with our faith. Before God healed me of my pessimism, I normally prayed for things that I could achieve on my own or seemed realistic for me to have in my future. Those prayers sounded something like this: "Lord, help me get an A in the test this week" and "Lord, bless me with a great job this summer." Albeit these requests were legitimate and God honored them, it didn't necessarily challenge my faith to grow. But at the time this was all the faith that I could muster.

While I believe God cares and is connected to the small things in our lives, He wants us to be audacious in our prayer requests. He wants us to ask Him for things that we think are absolutely impossible for us to achieve. When we don't have faith to ask God for something big, God is committed to growing our faith until we can. God likes to start right where you are. He might take those small requests that you could achieve on your own and allow the circumstances in your life to grow so challenging that the small prayer requests now seem impossible to achieve.

I call this growing your faith in reverse.

Let me give you an example and use Abraham again. God didn't give Abraham a difficult promise to believe in. He gave him a simple one: you will have a son. Having a baby was common, expected and...possible for Abraham and Sarah to achieve on their own. But God allowed years of infertility, disappointment, famine, moving from one place to another and failure to be included in their journey. Year after year the decline of their physical bodies and strength made having a baby seem unlikely. After a while, what seemed like a simple promise to fulfill now seemed impossible.

Getting To Impossible

I remember the first time I was challenged to believe God for the impossible. I was a freshman in college and wanted a car. At the time it was no big deal. All my friends had one and I was working several jobs to save enough to buy a used one. But as I prayed, God challenged me to take my prayer request to the next level and ask Him for a brand-new car. Because I was new in my Christianity, my faith was pretty strong.

I immediately went out and started test driving and inquiring about purchasing a new car. But each dealership told me the same thing: you don't have enough credit, nor do you earn enough. I then went and solicited my parents for the money and realized they couldn't afford to put me through school and buy me a brand-new car. To make matters worse, because of my class schedule, I had to leave the job that I was working.

So now what appeared possible seemed improbable. Every year was more of the same. My credit application was denied and I was told "you don't have enough." Year after year I kept trying. My friends and family thought I was being bourgeoise. They said, "Just get a used car and trade it for a new one in a few years. Stop making it a big deal." But for some reason I couldn't explain the conviction I had to wait and trust God. By my senior year I was fully discouraged and frustrated. I too had decided that this was becoming a bigger deal than it needed to be. I had expected to have a car to drive to school. School would be over in a few months. What was the point in God making me wait?

Sometimes the way God grows your faith is to disappoint your expectations. He allows challenges and roadblocks to interrupt your progress. God will move the blessing that you want and that you have the power to get out of your reach, only to invite you to stretch for it again in a way that enlarges your faith and trust in Him. Right when I got to the point of giving up and buying a used car, I sensed God saying, "Look again." So I mustered up the courage to go back out again to the same dealership that denied me each year.

When I arrived, a new agent was working, and he said, "You should look at the new cars we just got in." I told him I didn't know if I would qualify. He looked at me and said, "You never know; just have faith." It was as if God was speaking to me at that very moment. In less than an hour, I had qualified for a brand-new car and drove it off the lot the next week.

Looking back, I realized that God used my small request to develop and increase my faith. He waited until things looked hopeless to energize my courage to trust Him for the impossible. This one experience became the foundation for a lifelong journey of learning how to walk in faith.

Try That Again

He did the same thing in Abraham's life. God waited until having a baby seemed impossible and unattainable for Abraham and Sarah. But at 90 and 100 years old, they were told by God to "try again." It was on that last try that God fulfilled a promise that seemed impossible. Have you given up on something because it didn't happen the first, second or third time? Does it feel impossible? If so, good. It means you're in the right position to believe for it again. This time, you will need to rely on God's strength and resources and not your own. You will need to muster all your courage to overcome the embarrassment, feelings of failure and hopelessness to give it one more go. Can you do it again? I think you can.

Here's the real fruit of Abraham's faith journey: if Abraham had produced children in his own strength, God would never have received the credit. Abraham may never have entered the "hall of faith," and you and I would not have a reference point to encourage ourselves when the season of waiting and wondering seems endless.

This is faith in reverse—when God takes our small dreams and enlarges our troubles to increase our faith. As a pessimist in recovery who has worked most of her life to grow in faith, I've watched God use small moments to enlarge my audacity and hope and produce a greater trust and praise for Him.

You may not have the faith to ask God for something impossible. But God meets you where you are. If it seems as if you've been unable to achieve even your small requests, it's possible that God is growing your faith...in reverse.

CHAPTER 7

RAISE YOUR CUP

"Don't get stuck on small. Don't stop dreaming,
reaching and enhancing what you have."
—TD Jakes

It might be hard to believe, but God wants you to ask Him for more. As a child, I was often discouraged from asking for more of anything. My parents were from the "old school" and believed we had to say "thank you" and "no thank you" even when we didn't feel that way. We also learned that the sign of gratefulness was not asking for more; it was being satisfied with what we had. I realize that my parents taught us this way because they struggled financially and wanted us to be independent.

But this isn't how God operates in His relationships with us. God desires that we ask Him for everything and recognize that He is the source of all our resources. While He may not always respond to our request with a yes, audacity in prayer is a lifestyle that moves us forward rather than a formula we use to get everything we pray for.

Discover Your Ask

God wants us to put our faith and trust in Him to fulfill a heaven-sized request. Your prayer requests are often in alignment with how you see yourself or your perception of how God sees you. If you don't see yourself as deserving of more, you won't ask for it. If you believe that God sees you as less than qualified, then your prayer requests will only echo your internal perception.

Your worship and praise will reflect your faith and sound something like these song lyrics I used to sing: "Any way you bless me, I'll be satisfied" and "All I want is you, Jesus." Don't get me wrong, these songs are good and virtuous, but they don't address the other aspects of your life where you hold certain wants or desires. Nor do these songs require any vulnerability or courage.

I was teaching a workshop a few years ago and asked the women, "What do you want?" Many of them responded by stating what they needed. I asked the question, "If all of your needs were met, what do you truly want and desire that you don't think you can have?" Silence permeated the room for about five minutes, and only a few answered the question with dreams and ideas that they desired to see fulfilled.

Sadly, many of us live our needs and not our dreams. We've been taught to ask for the basics and that's it. I often wonder if it's because we've heard too many sermons or messages about God providing our needs and not enough messages about Him fulfilling our desires. I keep a journal, and each year in January, I write down every specific prayer request that I want to see God fulfill for that year. As the year progresses, I get encouraged when I go back and see many of them answered.

So, what's your ask? What are you currently trusting God to do in your life? You should be asking God for something right now that makes your inner critic and pessimist scream in protest. You may be thinking that your dream or idea is so big and there are so many roadblocks to overcome that there's no use praying about it. But God is not intimidated by the size of your dream or the obstacles standing in the way of it. God doesn't look at opposition the way that we do. He sees these deterrents as opportunities to reveal His ability and power through you.

Experience Vs. Expectation

Disappointment, frustration and a life of struggle have a way of crippling your courage to ask God for things beyond your capability. I want to share with you a story in the Bible that exemplifies the courage to expect and ask for more. Acts 3:1-10 highlights a man who was born lame and was carried daily to a temple gate called Beautiful. Because of his handicap, tradition and law prevented him from entering the gate and attending the services. Many who were poor or sick stood close to the entrance of the gate and leaned on the benevolence of those worshippers going into the temple. This lame man was no exception, as the Bible says he was "expecting to receive something." Even though he had this expectation, it seems he accepted the idea of living outside the gate.

The fact that he never went through the gate is symbolic. Gates in the Bible often represent access, transition, and advancement. But his experience was limited to him receiving outside the gate. Therefore, he resigned himself on some level to being close to a place of breakthrough and advancement without hope of ever achieving it. As a therapist, I suspect that his physical handicap may have somehow affected his perception regarding what he could receive in life. While I believe he had a sense of faith because he showed up every day expecting to receive something, his physical limitations handicapped his faith into believing that he could not reach for anything beyond his experiences. Every day this lame man got close to entering a new dimension in his life but struggled to achieve it.

You may not have any physical handicaps, but I would guess there have been some experiences in your life that wounded you emotionally and spiritually—so much so that it convinced you to lower your expectations to what you could receive and achieve from life. These emotional and spiritual handicaps now prevent you from seeing yourself as worthy of receiving what God truly wants to give you.

Don't misunderstand or misconstrue the word "worthy," as none of us are worthy or deserving of anything but death due to our sinful nature. But Romans 5:1 says, "Therefore having been justified by faith we have peace with God through our Lord Jesus Christ, through whom we also have access by faith into this grace in which we stand and rejoice in the hope of the glory of God." God's declaration over us as being justified allows us to stand in Christ Jesus as forgiven and favored to re-ceive what God has purposed and planned for us.

I saw something familiar in the story of the lame man in my own life in that there were some painful experiences that didn't fully strip me of my faith but caused me to lower my expectations for what I could receive. You can become trapped in your experi-ences. Painful and negative experiences have a way of changing your perception and reshaping what you should expect out of life.

For example, if you grew up poor you may unconsciously gravitate toward a life of struggle. If you've experienced the men in your life as being absent, hurtful and unfaithful, it's possible that you will unintentionally recreate and repeat your history even if it goes against what you really expect and desire. Eventually your experiences will attack your expectation.

If I can be creative for a second, I can almost hear the argu-ment between experience and expectation when you try and believe God for something greater:

Expectation: "I'm going to see if I can get through the gate today. It just might work."

Experience: "Oh yeah? Well, don't get your hopes up! You know what happened yesterday when you got to the gate…you got close but never made it in."

Expectation: "I'm going to put in a resume for that job. I don't have the background, but I am believing God to give me favor."

Experience: "Really? Do you remember the last time you put your resume in for something you were unqualified for? They made you jump through all those hoops. They told you they 'loved you,' and then what happened? You got close but you didn't get it. Are you really going to try that again?"

Does this internal argument sound familiar? Have you ever stood in the valley with faith on one side and frustration on the other, both yelling at each other? If you're not careful, the voice of experience will silence the voice of faith. Experience will whisper a lie in your ear and say, "No one else in your family has money, so why would you think God wants to bless you with wealth?" or, "You do realize that no one is having a baby after forty years of age, right? Why are you still hoping to have children at this late stage?"

Experience will kidnap and hold a funeral service for your expectancy if you allow it to. We call this in counseling the "death of expectation." It's when you decide that it's useless to keep praying for things that may never come to pass. So you silently come to the conclusion that being single, sick, or broke must be God's will for you. You relinquish what you really want and settle for what you can get. Have you already concluded that it's safer to downgrade your expectation so you won't get disappointed? Are you settled with the idea of just being close to your dreams rather than taking a risk and reaching for something beyond your experience?

Cultivating Courage

My desire and conviction to start a women's ministry initially began with wanting to do a small women's breakfast. I prayed earnestly for God to bring fifty women to the event. Honestly, this was not a real faith leap for me. I had already recruited ten of my friends to be on the team and asked them to recruit five women each. No problem—I had this conference in the bag! But something changed once I signed the contract. I started to feel very uneasy. It was the kind of unrest that signaled God wanted to do something more.

As I prayed, I sensed God telling me to cancel the contract and get a bigger room. I quickly responded with "God, I don't have money for a larger room!" At the time, my husband had been unemployed for close to a year. We were living on food stamps and were about a month away from either foreclosing on our home or putting it up for short sale. I dutifully reminded God of this—as if He had forgotten. But as weeks passed, I felt the gentle pull of God wanting me to trust Him. So, with fear and a little faith, I went back to the venue and canceled the previous contract. The banquet manager said, "Are you sure you want to do this? You know you're going to have to guarantee financially over double the original amount, right?"

It's easy to walk in faith when there's no risk. When I had my friends helping me recruit women, launching the business seemed like a piece of cake. But God moved the goal and asked me to stretch for more with no guarantee of how things would work out. This is how God cultivates courage. He creates a risk without promising what the outcome will be.

I wish I could tell you that I answered the banquet manager with boldness and said, "Listen, my God shall supply all my needs according to His riches in glory," or, "Greater is He that is in me than He that is in the world." But instead, I weakly nodded my head yes, signed the contract and cried from fear when I returned to my car.

I had faith and the expectation that I was supposed to launch this business. But my faith was situated at the level of my lameness and not at the level of my potential in God. Meaning, I placed my faith and courage in the same place as my resources. I was broke and couldn't pay the bills, so I reached for what I thought I could achieve with the resources I had. But God doesn't want us to reach for what we think we can achieve based on our limited resources on earth. He wants us to reach for what we don't think we can get and trust in His never-ending supply in heaven.

It takes audacity to step beyond your limitations and deficits and have an expectation for something greater. You need courage to overcome all the hurts and disappointments in your life that contributed to you being lame in your faith, expectation, vision or passion. Additionally, walking in courage requires a vulnerability in asking and expecting something that God just might say no to.

Reach For It Anyway

Let's be honest, I'm sure there were times when you stepped out in boldness and courage to accomplish a goal or plan, or you prayed for God to grant you a miracle or open a door. You had the faith and conviction that it was God moving you in that direction. But the answer was no and the door remained closed. That experience put a wall around your heart, and you quietly decided to lower your expectation. You may have even decided to not ask God for anything else to prevent future disappointment.

But here's the reality: while God's answer may be "no" or silence, He still wants us to take the risk of faith anyway. He wants us to raise our expectations and see Him through the lens of our faith and not through the lens of our frustrations, limitations or fears. Here's another truth I learned: sometimes God's "no" is His way of saying "not yet" rather than "never." Either way, we are being called to ask and reach for things we don't think we can achieve.

After signing the new contract, I expected God to reward my faith with instant results. But the registration numbers were incredibly slow, several team members resigned at the last minute and it didn't seem that people were that interested in attending. For months I agonized and doubted my decision. I got mad at God and promised myself I would never do it again. Yes, my inner pessimist was at work. But what I love about God is He didn't require me to feel faith—just act on it.

If you're waiting for the feeling of faith to arrive before you move, you will be waiting for a long time. Faith and courage are more than feelings—they're actions. Somewhere in between complete anxiety and despair, God's faithfulness to His promise showed up. An explosion occurred a few days before the event in that it seemed every woman in that county and beyond couldn't get a ticket fast enough. Not only did I meet my contract obligation, but I exceeded it. I stood back and watched God do something miraculous with a decision I chose to say yes to. To this day, IGNITE draws hundreds of women from literally around the country, and it started with me having the audacity to reach for more.

Leaping Into More

Even though this lame man in Acts resigned himself to living outside the gate, when he saw Peter and John, the Bible tells us he was "expecting to receive something." Peter and John were well known and astute members of the Jewish community. I could be taking creative license when I shouldn't, but I believe in order to get their attention he had to raise his cup a little higher than he was used to doing. This required him to stretch. It meant he would need to forget about how lame and limited he was and reach for something beyond him.

Can you raise your cup and stretch your faith to ask for something that doesn't match your location in life, education, background or experiences? This is what God wants from you. When you raise your cup, what you receive will always be greater than what you hoped. In Acts 3:6, Peter told the lame man, "Silver or gold I do not have, but what I do have I give you. In the name of Jesus Christ of Nazareth, walk." They took his hand and helped him up, and not only did he walk again, but he began to leap and jump. I'm certain he probably never imagined walking again, let alone leaping. His one act of courage accelerated what he hoped for or imagined.

I get it. You're reading this and saying, "Niki, you don't know how many roadblocks and closed doors I've faced. You have no clue how many times I've received a 'no.' I just don't think I can keep holding on to hope." Sometimes God's "no" is meant to prepare you for a bigger "yes. Disappointment is designed to develop your faith. It's possible that what you've been asking and expecting was too small. God is not interested in blessing you with what you had in mind. He wants to bless you with what He has in mind. God's blessings are always exceedingly and abundantly more than we can ask or think.

Here is one final lesson to point out from this story: in order for Peter to raise him up, the lame man probably had to release the cup he was holding on to. I see the power of audacity in this. The cup was a sign of his comfort zone. It's the one thing he owned that defined his daily success. It was his strategy to getting his needs met. It was safe, secure and predictable.

But Peter and John invited him to let go of what he knew and take a leap into the unknown. The lame man was healed because he chose to embrace courage over comfort. He decided to be audacious in letting go of his limitations rather than accepting his fate in life and holding on to his restraints. In other words, he reached for the miraculous instead of the mundane.

You may be waiting on God to open a door and release something you've been praying and hoping for. But what if He is waiting on you to raise your cup and reach for it instead? Your time for waiting outside the gate is over. You don't have to settle for safe or for less than what you deserve. If you're willing, God wants to give you the strength to let go of the past and leap through the doorway that's already open for you.

PART 4
AUDACITY TO
LOOK AGAIN

CHAPTER 8

THE POWER OF PERSPECTIVE

*"Your greatest challenge is not the barrier—it's
what you tell yourself about the barrier."*
—*Niki Brown*

Have you ever wondered how two siblings can come out of the same house—with the exact same rules and parenting structure—but one sibling will declare that their childhood was wonderful, while the other will say the exact opposite? Or how two business leaders can experience a similar downturn in the economy, but one will rise and the other will fall? Why is one able to rise past the challenges and become successful, while the other struggles through them? I don't believe it's due to a lack of intelligence or the fact that one of them faced less challenges than the other but rather how each of them perceived those challenges.

It's called perspective. It's powerful because it governs your world. It's the filter through which you see the world.

Everything in your environment plays a role in shaping your filter, from your culture, religion, tradition, and rules to your disappointments and past hurts. In turn, your filter determines your decisions and ultimately your destiny. Perspective shapes your reality. It determines what you see and believe. You may have heard the sayings "If you look for the good, you will find it" or "You can find the bad in anything if you look hard enough." Like a camera, your perspective has the power to look at life through any lens you choose.

John Lubbock (British statesman, 1834-1913) said in his book The Beauties of Nature and the Wonders of the World We Live In, "What we do see depends mainly on what we look for. In the same field the farmer will notice the crop, the geologists the fossils, botanists the flowers, artists the coloring, sportsmen the cover for the game. Though we may all look at the same things, it does not all follow that we should see them."

The beauty in this passage is twofold. First, it shows how perspective makes you unique. How you see things and what you see is inherent in the diversity of who you are, where you're from and even where you are going. You bring that gift with you to every situation, problem and opportunity. Second, the field is not limited to one person's interpretation and viewpoint. The field is diverse in its ability and function. It can produce and create on many levels. But for that to happen the farmer must be willing to shift his focus and lens.

The farmer may never be a botanist or an agriculturalist and can only see the field through the lens of his passion and purpose, which is to grow crops. But if he's wise, he will adjust his lens to see the field has a greater capacity to do more. This is the problem most of us have with perspective. We isolate it. We tend to believe that our viewpoint is the only one that exists. And while what you see may be your truth, it's not the only truth.

Adjust Your Lens

Your life is similar to the field in that you are not singular in purpose or potential. You have the capacity to grow and accomplish things beyond your own expectations and vision. Sometimes you can miss seeing your own multifacetedness if you get stuck on your limitations and the ones that others put on you. So it's important that you audit the lens through which you view life. What is your perspective? What type of lens do you look through daily and which lens do you bring to circumstances that are challenging to you?

I told you a few chapters ago that I struggled with pessimism. So when I took my own inventory, I was not surprised to find that my lens was pessimism and fear. While I am getting a lot better, I'm still a work in progress. The pessimism lens consistently looks for things to be negative and will seek out the worst in people and situations. The problem with perspective is you will find what you're looking for. When I looked for the negative, I found it. If I anticipated that people would reject me, somehow I found a way to be offended.

My focus on the negative also carried into how I handled difficult circumstances. A few years ago, my husband and I hit a rough patch financially. He lost his six-figure job, and I was only working part-time. In my quest to become less pessimistic and more positive, I chose not to fret. But as the weeks turned into months…and months, I couldn't hold back the dark clouds of doubt and negativity. My perspective shifted from "This is just a test" to "God is trying to destroy us! He doesn't care about us. If He did, we wouldn't be in this situation."

What I couldn't perceive was how God was using this occasion to develop us and not destroy us. Had I shifted my focus, I may have sensed that God's greater purpose was to take us through a season of cutback and loss so we could refocus on things that were less material and more spiritual, such as prayer, devotion, and greater commitment to each other.

Is your lens out of focus and causing God and life to look distorted? Have you stepped over the wheat growing in the field because you're too focused on the weeds? God allows opportunity and opposition to grow in the same space. The ground that carries the dirt also holds the seed. If you focus on the dirt, you will miss the destiny that's hidden in the seed. If you don't intentionally adjust your lens through which you view life's circumstances, you will miss the beauty in the brokenness. You won't understand how God can use a difficult season and turn it into the launching pad for your future.

Look Again

Sometimes you have to look again. In my opinion this is audacious, daring living. This type of courage may not appear to be on the same scale as believing God for a miracle or literally taking a step in the natural by faith, but you'll be surprised how much strength it takes to step back in the middle of chaos, disappointment and confusion and see life through a different lens.

There's a story in the Bible I believe illustrates the courage of one woman who decided to shift her perspective in a painful situation. In the book of John 20:1-16, the apostle John recounts the story of Mary Magdalene who came to the tomb after Jesus' crucifixion and burial. To understand the context of this passage: Jesus had only been in ministry for three years before He was crucified. To those who followed Him, His death was sudden, unexpected and too soon. For Mary and the disciples, He was their long-awaited Messiah, the one expected to restore power to the Jews and to set up an earthly kingdom to rule. So when He was crucified, the disappointment and hopelessness that followed were felt among those who believed in Him.

I'm sure Jesus' death challenged their perspectives and faith in who He claimed to be and all the signs He performed. I can imagine them quietly wondering, Was Jesus really the Messiah? If so, why was He crucified? Was that really God's will? Were the miracles and signs that Jesus performed even authentic? How come He didn't save Himself and us like the Scriptures foretold?

Have you ever gone through a time when the dreams and goals you expected to grow were cut off, or the plans you hoped to see fulfilled went unrealized? You met someone perfect for you, and you had expectations of getting married. But for some reason the relationship ended, and you can't understand why. Or maybe you finally received your dream job—the one you cried over, prayed for and worked hard to receive. But you were laid off six months later and have struggled ever since to get realigned with what God wants for you.

Mary's faith was crushed along with her dreams for her future, which is why she didn't come to the gravesite of Jesus expecting to see Him risen. Her perspective was on what she had lost—not on what she was about to gain. But when she got to the tomb, the stone had been rolled away, and she assumed that someone had stolen the body of Jesus. While Jesus had spoken frequently about His death, burial and resurrection, none of the disciples embraced or understood it. So when the disciples showed up, they all looked into the tomb and saw the grave cloths with no body. The disciples walked away, probably assuming as well that His body had been taken.

But not Mary. Mary doesn't walk away from the tomb. She is determined to see Jesus. Here is where audacious and daring faith shows up. Mary takes the risk and goes back—to look again. This time she sees angels in white sitting on the bedside of Jesus and inquires of them His whereabouts. In another account, these angels tell her that Jesus has risen.

What a shock this must have been to Mary. She came prepared to memorialize someone who had died, only to discover that what she had lost and loved had been resurrected. If Mary had walked away like the disciples and hadn't taken the courage to look again, she would have missed seeing Jesus, who was disguised as the gardener.

A Garden In The Grave

How often do we miss seeing Jesus in our circumstances? Like the disciples, sometimes we walk away too soon. The garden of Gethsemane and Jesus's tomb were in the same location. If you become too focused on what's lying in the grave, you will miss what God has waiting for you in the garden. Sometimes the blessing comes disguised as a burden.

You may have experienced some disappointing times that challenged your faith. But I'm a firm believer that God uses disappointment to develop your vision to see what's on the other side of destiny. Here's what was on the other side for Mary and the disciples: they were about to learn that death no longer had the power to snatch away the hopes and dreams of His people forever. Christ holds the resurrecting power of eternal life.

Are you walking away from something that God is about to resurrect? Are you so focused on the hurt and pain of what you lost that you are unable to see what God is releasing for you to gain? God wants to use your heartbreak to change your perspective of your possibilities. He can only do it if you choose to see that in every graveyard there is a garden that exists.

The truth is this: God's presence in your life is not always designed to fix your problems or cart them away, but it is intended to change your perspective of the problem. This was true for Moses and the nation of Israel who were trying to escape Pharaoh and the land of Egypt. They didn't know how they would get across the Red Sea. Pharaoh's army was close behind them, and all Moses had as a line of defense was a stick.

But it wasn't the Red Sea or the rod that was holding Moses back from his deliverance. It was Moses' perspective of the Red Sea. It was the nation's fear that the Red Sea would destroy their dreams of freedom. But God challenged Moses to look again and realize the same sea that had the potential to drown them was the same sea God would use to deliver them.

Let's get back to Mary. While Mary didn't recognize that a resurrection had taken place and that Jesus had probably been in the garden the whole time, what I love about her courage is that she stayed in position. Mary didn't quit. This is what audacity looks like. It's choosing not to abandon the place of disappointment and brokenness when you have a legitimate reason to walk away.

It's remaining resilient until what you're hoping to see actually comes to pass. When you do this, you will discover what Mary found—angels in the tomb, which signifies not only that heaven is connected to your pain but also that in place of your deepest disappointments, God will give you another perspective of His will and purpose. Mary's reward was that she got to see more than expected. She got to experience more of God's goodness than she hoped for as she made history in becoming the first person and woman to witness the miracle of Christ's resurrection.

I don't know what you abandoned or walked away from because of disappointment, rejection or discouragement, but I challenge you to look again. Some of the best things that will ever take place in your life are found when you change the lens through which you're viewing your circumstance.

It's only then that you can see how God has more working for you than against you.

CHAPTER 9
DESTINY IN THE DETAILS

"No matter where you are on your journey,
that's exactly where you need to be. The
next road is always ahead."
—*Oprah Winfrey*

A few years ago, Harold and I moved to North Carolina.
He received an amazing offer, and we decided to take the
leap. It was bittersweet as it meant putting our gorgeous home
that we had just built on the market to sell. When we toured
the area, I was intent on finding something that looked and
felt like the home we left. This seemed next to impossible, but
after a few agonizing days of searching, we found something we
could settle on.

Right before we signed the lease, Harold sensed my quiet
dissatisfaction. Because he knows how fickle I am, he asked if I
was happy with the house and if it's what I really wanted. I told
him the home wasn't as big as the one we left and proceeded
to show him all the areas that were considerably smaller in

comparison to our old home. He said, "Actually this house is bigger. The builder added extra space to the bedrooms versus hallway and living space." It struck me as odd that I hadn't noticed this. I pay close attention to details, yet here I was in a new place with more room, but missed it. I learned an important lesson that day on perspective: when you're too focused on what was, you really can't appreciate what is. I had grown so enamored with my last home that I couldn't see that God had transitioned me to a better place.

How often have I done this? How many times have I failed to enjoy the blessing of being in a new place because I was too focused on where I had been? What I've come to understand is we are either looking forward or backward. The sermons or inspirational messages we listen to point us toward letting go of the past or dreaming forward.

These are all good, as we need that motivation to fulfill our purpose. But what about now? How do you embrace the everyday "what is"? On top of that, how do you plan for what's next when you're struggling through the difficulty of a divorce, sickness, or other circumstance that feels beyond your control? Sometimes the real challenge is not in moving forward or letting go of yesterday. It's in learning how to embrace today.

The temptation to abandon where you are for greener pastures is real. And yes, there are times when you need to transition into a more conducive environment to grow and thrive. But sometimes God's will is being unfolded right where you are. Most often our problem is that we have trouble seeing destiny in our present reality. For instance, you may have a dream of owning your own business, but right now you're working as a receptionist. From your viewpoint, you're just answering phones and delivering the mail. You can't see how the dream of being an entrepreneur will come to pass in your present position. The reason you can't see it is because God doesn't unfold the dream in your life all at once.

I like to use the analogy of a puzzle. The outside of the box has the picture of the puzzle—but inside it's broken apart in pieces. I never liked working on puzzles, as they're painstakingly slow, but this is how God's big picture for your life unfolds. It shows up in pieces, and God slowly puts those pieces together. Each step and season you go through is another piece of the puzzle God is connecting into place.

So if you're looking for God's big picture in your everyday routine, you won't find it. I'm not saying it doesn't exist. It does. You just can't see it. Little by little God's will is working behind the scenes and coming together in the mundane moments and obscure opportunities in life.

Nurture Your Now

Our problem is we spend too much energy and focus on trying to escape those moments where it feels as if nothing is happening. So we start reaching and yearning for tomorrow when we haven't exhausted today. The popular term for this is called "destination disease." It's the belief that happiness is waiting for you the moment you meet the right person, graduate from school, make a certain income or live a certain lifestyle. So we put our lives on hold, waiting for "someday" to come. The church soliloquy "I'm just waiting for my season to come" reinforces the idea that there's something we're missing in today.

While I believe God has greater things in store for us, every season is "your season." Every moment is a seed. There is potential for growth in whatever season or circumstance you find yourself in. Think about the journey of the acorn into a tree. Its growth is predicated on being buried and hidden in the dirt. Its environment isn't the most comfortable, but it's the most conducive to helping the acorn reach its maximum potential.

While you may not like the moment you're in because it's uncomfortable, difficult or moving too slow, it's a moment designed by God to fit into a larger purpose for your life. What I'm saying is if you don't nurture now, you will never get to next. If you don't believe in now, you will not prepare for what's next.

A story in Matthew 25:14-30 illustrates this. Jesus shares a parable with His disciples on the importance of being good stewards by using the example of a businessman who gives each of his servants gold coins, which were called "talents," to invest. One was given five, another was given two and the last was given one. The servant with five talents went and invested them and received five more. The one with two did the same. When the businessman returns, he says to both, "Well done, good and faithful servant! You've been faithful with a few things; I will put you in charge of many things."

But the servant who was only given one talent took it and hid it in the ground. He told the business owner, "Master, I knew you to be a hard man, reaping where you did not sow, and gathering where you scattered no seed, so I was afraid, and I went and hid your talent in the ground. Here, you have what is yours." But the business owner answered him, "You wicked and slothful servant! You knew that I reap where I have not sown and gather where I scattered no seed? Then you ought to have invested my money with the bankers, and at my coming I should have received what was my own with interest."

My suspicion is that the servant got stuck on how small his talent was and concluded that it probably couldn't help him get to where he wanted to go in life. So instead of growing the talent into something more, which would take time and patience, he abandoned it. But he didn't understand the principle of the seed. A tiny seed in your hand never looks like the tree it will become. It has to be buried in the dirt, hidden in the dark and cultivated in order for it to explode into its potential. If you disregard the seed because of its size, you will miss its future harvest.

Have you buried away talents that were designed to be a harvest for your future? Are you waiting on something more to come when you haven't done anything with what you have right now? To get promoted to where you want to go, you must master where you are. Your resources and gifts are only small now because they're waiting on you to grow them. To qualify for the next level, you must become an expert in your field. It doesn't matter if that "field" is as small as a part-time job or an opportunity that feels menial or a position where you are overqualified. The next blessing God wants to give you is contingent on you outgrowing the blessing you currently occupy.

God doesn't waste tears, effort or faith. Whatever God has you working on right now is purposeful. Stick with the process. Unpack your patience and use it for this journey. Don't become so enthralled with the promise that you neglect your progress. The launching pad you need to propel you into your next dream home, job or opportunity isn't going to just show up. You have to build it. Right where you are—right now.

Opportunity in Opposition

I don't want to downplay the fact that your life may be very challenging and your goal is to get into a better place. I want to expound on a point I mentioned in the previous chapter. God allows opportunity and opposition to share the same space in your life. Your season will not be void of strife and tension. Conflict will always be present in a place of goodness. But here's the key: the one you focus on the most is the one that will grow the most.

So the question is, are you focusing on the opposition (how difficult things are and how everything is going haywire in your life right now), or are you looking at the opportunities (the blessing God has hidden in disguise)? You may be asking, "Okay, what opportunities? What blessings? I sure don't feel blessed, nor can I see how God is working." Here's another parable that may help you see it:

In Matthew 13:25, Jesus tells His disciples that the kingdom of heaven is like a man who sowed good seed in his field, and while men slept, an enemy came and sowed weeds among the wheat. When the crops began to grow and produce grain, the weeds grew too. The servants of the owner said to him, "Didn't you plant good seed? Where did the weeds come from?" The owner replied, "An enemy has done this." The servants then asked the owner, "Do you want us to pull them up?" He replied, "No, because while you are pulling up the weeds, you may uproot the wheat. Let them both grow together."

As far as the servants were concerned, the weeds represented a roadblock to the wheat's ability to grow. The most logical remedy was to uproot and get rid of them. But the landowner recognized something else. He understood that even though the opposition was present, there was an opportunity for the wheat to grow and thrive. You may be viewing the current trouble in your life as an obstacle that will prevent you from moving forward. This causes you to focus all your efforts on uprooting it. You're doing everything you can to fix the problems you see in your business, family or ministry with no real progress.

But here's a news flash: the presence of weeds will not stop your wheat. In fact, uprooting weeds can kill the wheat if their roots are intertwined. Just like every garden needs manure to thrive, you need the presence of conflict and tension to grow. But if you focus solely on the problem (weeds), you will miss the promise (wheat) that's growing right beside it.

You will miss how God is using every obstacle as an opportunity for you to grow, trust, and develop your faith. You won't see that it's actually your harvest season—which is a time of celebration, increase and restoration. But isn't that what the

Niki Brown

devil is hoping for? He wants you so focused and inundated with fighting the opposition in your marriage, job and circumstances that you miss the blessing that's waiting for you in the middle of it. He wants you to feel discouraged in a season where you should be excited and hopeful.

Grace To Grow

God doesn't want you to run from the conflict but to grow through it. And just as the saying goes, "There is an app for that," there is a grace for that. There is a grace God gives that equips us to exercise courage in difficult times. In Ephesians 4:7, Paul says, "But to each one of us grace has been given as Christ apportioned it." I don't believe God allows opposition, heartbreak, struggle and pain to show up in your life if He hasn't given you a grace to grow through it.

Our response to God's grace should be to exercise audacious faith in our season of struggle. What does this mean? It means having a faith and a focus to look beyond adversity to see a bigger promise ahead. Better yet, it means having the audacity to plan and prepare for a future promise while we're still wrestling with the circumstances of today. When God gives you a grace to grow, you can learn to stand your ground even when you are frustrated and feeling hopeless. You can also believe that you will not be defeated or uprooted away from the place God has ordained you to thrive in.

Okay this all sounds inspiring but you might be wondering, "How do I actually grow through tough times. How do I

76

nurture my now?" Prayer is always the obvious answer but if you're like me you learn through instruction. So here are some intentional courageous steps you can take in order to thrive in the midst of opposition:

Pick your battles. The natural response when you're in a season of struggle is to fight. Some of us fight quicker than others. While the bible encourages us to "fight the good fight of faith," it doesn't mean you should fight every battle. The challenge is determining which battles to jump in and which ones to ignore. Unfortunately many of us tend to pick the wrong battles to fight. Those are the fights which have no resolution and leaves you more hurt, confused and upset than you started.

Sometimes you just need to save your energy. Fighting everything and everyone is exhausting. Jumping on social media to air out your grievances creates a cycle of drama that will drain you emotionally. Choosing to be quiet when everything in you wants to argue, curse and scream is not a sign surrender. It's an act of courage. It's an indication that you believe God is going to fight this battle for you. So before you engage in the next battle ask yourself, "Do I *need* to fight this? If so why? Will this battle bring resolution or more confusion? Will this upset my peace?" If so, disengage. Throw down your weapons and recognize that God is inviting you to watch Him move on your behalf.

Plan around your possibilities. Growing through opposition requires you to look beyond the trouble and take advantage of the time to nurture your opportunities. I mentioned a few chapters ago that my husband and I hit a financial rough patch several years ago. It also seemed as if my ministry had come to a complete halt. I was not receiving any calls to speak or opportunities to counsel and coach as I had previously.

After several months of sulking God impressed upon my heart to dig up all the talents I had buried and do something more with them. I wiped off the dust on my old journal books and found pages of thoughts, ideas and plans I had never utilized. These were new possibilities that I could step into. But I first needed to believe that my season of opposition would eventually end. I had to shift my focus from my financial woes and wondering *if* God was going to bring us out—to planning for *when* He brought us out.

One of the challenges to growing and nurturing your now is the ability to *see* your possibilities in where you are. It's having the faith to believe your season of struggle is not permanent but temporary. I encourage you to use this time to dig up the talents you've hidden, dreams you've cast aside, book ideas you haven't put to paper and choose to *grow*! When you plan around your possibilities you're exercising faith that a "next" is coming.

Practice gratitude. I've always struggled with being grateful. Most pessimist do. We tend to focus on the things that are going wrong and struggle to see the good. On some level I believed that if expressed gratitude I was settling or communicating that everything was great. But gratefulness is not settling for what is nor does it indicate your approval of challenging times. Gratitude points your focus in a different direction.

While you're not ignoring the trouble you're choosing to center your attention on the areas of God's goodness. Gratefulness is your way of telling God you still trust Him and see His hand moving in your life in spite of the circumstances. Find the areas in your life that are going well. Create a list and post it on your mirror or a door so each day you are reminded of God's favor and presence in your life.

Not everything that brings conflict is an enemy to your growth. Sometimes trouble is a tutor. It teaches us how to shift our vision inward and even upward. The moment you stop fighting your perceived enemies around you, you will be able to nurture the gift, vision and dreams within you. When your focus turns inward, you will inevitably realize that the people and places you thought you needed to grow and survive, you can do without. You may also discover a tenacity and courage to endure things you never thought you could endure.

And most importantly you'll probably realize certain truths were in front of you all along, just like I figured out that the extra space I was longing for in my new home was there from the beginning.

The destiny was in the details.

PART 5
AUDACITY TO
WALK AWAY

CHAPTER 10

IF IT AIN'T BROKE, BREAK IT

*"Just try new things. Don't be afraid. Step out
of your comfort zones and soar, all right?"*
—Michelle Obama

I hope you recognize by now that audacity doesn't just influence your attitude but also impacts your belief system. Living audaciously begins from the inside and moves outward. It involves more than just daring acts which are visible to the outside world. It includes daring decisions that could expose you to more hurt, disappointment and rejection. It could also propel you into a life that's beyond your imagination.

I'm sure you've heard the saying "If it ain't broke, don't fix it," right? It's an outdated idiom, but the message holds a contemporary thought that still impacts the trajectory of your life goals and dreams. The belief behind it is if something is working well, it's probably best not to change it or else you could make things worse. From a leadership perspective, there is wisdom in this saying as it forces you to think about what's working in your organization, ministry, or business. One of the pitfalls in leading organizations through change is not understanding their unique positions to make necessary improvements for growth to occur.

Companies use an analyst tool called "SWOT," which stands for Strengths, Weaknesses, Opportunities and Threats, to assess and evaluate their organization as a whole and to identify the internal and external factors that can either help or hinder them from achieving their goals. I think anyone with a dream or ambition should do her own evaluation of her personal life as well. We can get so busy that we forget to put our lives on pause in order to really evaluate what we're doing and how well we are doing it.

Break Your Comfort Zone

Several years ago, I was working as an associate pastor at a very large church in New Jersey. I loved the job and the ability to work alongside believers, helping them achieve their goals and the vision of the church. I literally immersed myself in the work and gave everything to it. When my ten-year anniversary came around, I vividly remember the feeling of shock and bewilderment at how quickly time had passed. But I also began to reflect on where I was and where I wanted to be.

I realized that the satisfaction I was supposed to feel was missing. I couldn't put my finger on why I felt this way, as I had created over eight new programs/ministries, developed and managed more than thirty-forty leaders, oversaw and managed a counseling department, plus traveled and spoke weekly at conferences and events around the region. I had done more in those ten years than I ever could have imagined. So what was missing? Somehow I had shifted into a place of restlessness. Little by little I started to dread going into work and facing the monotony of doing the same thing in the same place every day.

I knew I probably needed a change, but where would I go? What would I do? Inherently I loved serving and working with people in that capacity. Even though there were some differences and certain drawbacks with the organization, I wasn't naive enough to think I would feel better in another company doing the same thing. Thus, my dilemma: I wanted to break free, yet I didn't have a justifiable reason to do so. In other words, nothing was broke, so why was I trying to fix it?

One of the greatest challenges to living audaciously is making a decision that puts you against the grain. Many of us have been taught to "go with the flow" and "leave well enough alone." But what if your heart and passion are not headed in the same direction as the "go with the flow" crowd? What if you don't want "well enough" but instead desire to have an extraordinary life and make an exceptional impact wherever you go? And finally, why on earth does something have to be broken for positive change to occur?

It's not your challenges that hinder you. It's the temptation to live within the status quo. You can become so comfortable in success that it blinds you to the other dimensions that exist within you. It's easy to remain in the status quo because it has a huge supportive network. You won't find too many proponents of change in this group. There will always be more voices advocating for you to stay than to go. You'll hear things like, "Girl, you should be grateful. If I had your life, I would be so happy. You're so successful at what you do. Why would you walk away to start all over again? Are you crazy? How old are you, anyway?" If you listen to the majority long enough, you will end up at a place of "no decision" and miss the opportunity to transition.

The only way to hit the next button in your life is to break what's not broken. This sounds a little cliché, but let me explain it this way: you will need to break the pattern of predictability to achieve the next-level results that you desire. In other words, you're not going to receive something new by doing something old.

Here is where you need audacity: when you choose to walk away from something that's working for no other reason than "it's time." That's it. You're not walking away because you are angry or things have gotten crazy and dysfunctional. It's simply time. Your desire to discover and embrace something new outweighs your need to stay comfortable.

Destiny and Disruption

Joshua Gans, an economist at the Rotman School of Management in Toronto and author of The Disruption Dilemma, writes that "firms fail because they keep making the same choices that made them successful. When successful organizations stick to their once-triumphant strategies, even as the world changes around them they eventually become irrelevant." Why? How does a company that was once successful suddenly become irrelevant?Because the next level of success demands that the organization remakes itself and creates a structure that has the capacity to handle innovation and change.

This plays out no differently in your life. In order to enter a new season, you must abandon old strategies that led you into predictable places—even if those places gave you great success. You then must be willing to transform and transition yourself in a way necessary to handle the new opportunities, relationships and assignments that God wants to give you.

Change requires a disruption. Destiny demands disruption. You can only embrace a destiny bigger than yourself when you allow God to interrupt your pattern of predictability—doing the same thing in the same way and achieving the same results. There is a familiar pattern that you have constructed in your life that needs to be dismantled for a change to occur. The interruption may need to take place in your relationships, the type of people you connect with, how you respond to anxiety or new challenges, or the way you go about accomplishing your goals.

While this sounds simple, it's also frightening. Disruption is easier said than done. Our patterns serve us. Those strategies which we see as foolproof and weather-resistant make us feel safe. Even if those patterns are dysfunctional, we experience a payout from doing things that keep us comfortable in what we know. But interrupting patterns, means you have to upset the applecart.

If you're a control freak (in recovery) like I am, not having the information on what's next is disconcerting. Not being able to control the outcome (although you never really could) will make you question everything you thought you knew and understood. You may even enter a period of doubting your own abilities, gifts, and self-worth. This explains why change may be met with resistance. But I'm learning that while radical change creates an upheaval that we fear, it also produces a transformation that we need.

Currently as I am writing this book, our entire nation and world is in the midst of a pandemic called COVID-19. In the blink of an eye, everything has been interrupted. Schools, churches, businesses and communities have been shuttered. Uncertainty, panic and anxiety have become the emotional norm. Our ability to interact and connect has completely changed with the government requirement of "social distancing" to prevent further transmission. Economists are now predicting a recession worse than what the nation experienced over ten years ago.

While it's frustrating to experience the "not knowing" aspect of how things will end, I'm a firm believer that none of this is a surprise to God. The current disruption plays into His bigger plans and destinies for us. The evidence is being seen now. Communities are uniting together. Families are being forced to connect and relate in ways that they haven't previously been able to due to busyness and technology. Businesses and churches found innovative ways to engage their customers and parishioners.

In disrupting the pattern God is transforming the familiar. You know the idiom "familiarity breeds contempt"? We now have an opportunity to express new appreciation for things we have taken for granted and to transform. It's only when we allow God to interrupt our norms that we're able to grow beyond where we are and step into the next best versions of ourselves.

Don't Build A Memorial

Seven years ago I decided to walk away from the life I knew into one that was unfamiliar. Harold had been laid off from work, and within months we went from making six figures to living on food stamps. Life was completely interrupted. After waiting and wondering for about a year, he was offered an amazing job in Kentucky to operate as the CEO of a new healthcare organization. The joy and excitement of him receiving this offer were eclipsed by the uncertainty and fear of moving to a new location with no family or friends for miles.

Out of the two of us, I had the greatest resistance, as I struggled to believe that God would want me to give up everything to go and start again. While I had been feeling restless about my current position and really had a passion to leave, this wasn't how I had envisioned things happening. My unwillingness to say yes to the move brought several nights of conflict and tension between us. I spiritualized my fear by telling Harold that God had something better for him and maybe we should just wait.

In the meantime, the organization was waiting for us to make a decision, and I knew it came down to me. As I was taking my morning walk and weeping about the possibility of leaving everything, I sensed God asking, "Do you trust Me?" His question was really a statement, as God already knew the answer. It was also a revelation of my faith and the struggle to let go. I didn't trust Him. I didn't believe that I could walk away and still be me.

But maybe that was the point. He wanted me to be greater than who I was. That meant leaving the place that kept me comfortable. It led me to wonder if I had created an identity around a place and position versus my purpose and calling. Somewhere along the way I developed a misperception that I couldn't be successful beyond where I was. I believed that my accomplishments had less to do with my gifting (*the imposter syndrome at work*) and more to do with the people and place that gave me the title and position.

If I were to walk away I would leave all of that and me behind. None of those things were true but it's what kept me trapped and afraid to leave the familiar. I had built a monument around a season of success that I didn't believe I could replicate anywhere else.

If you hang around what you know for too long, you will create a memorial out of a moment that was designed to be temporary. This time in your life is just a moment. It may be one of your best moments and that's wonderful. Enjoy this season. Embrace the feeling of accomplishment. But don't memorialize it. God has something better.

The Road To Execeptional

What do you need to break in order for you to get to better? It could be your routine. Or maybe it's your mindset on how you envision things happening in your life. What would it mean for you to leave what's familiar to experience something new, or walk away from a relationship that's served its purpose in your life? Your success is not tied exclusively to a place—it's connected to who you are. My good friend Kim Woods said to me, "Niki when you carry greatness inside of you, it goes wherever you go."

Yes, I hear you. You're saying, "What I'm doing is working for me...and right now everything is going good." Believe me, I'm certainly not advocating for you to quit your job or ministry tomorrow. I'm also not trying to get you to abandon the strategies that are working for you. I'm here to challenge your perspective for you to see how those strategies which got you to good may not get you to exceptional. I'm shaking the cage of complacency you might be hiding in and challenging the status quo areas of your life in order for you to get to more.

You may not know what "exceptional" looks like right now and that's okay. But I encourage you to dig deep and grab the courage necessary to identify those areas that have served your comfort zone for too long. Your ability to move forward into the next level of faith and success depends on it.

CHAPTER 11

DIVORCE YOUR PLANS

*"Never be so faithful to your plan that you are
unwilling to consider the unexpected."*
—Elizabeth Warren

Most of us can admit that our lives haven't gone exactly as
expected. As I child, I remember writing in my journal
about my various dreams for the future, which included how I
was going to become a criminal investigator, marry the man of
my dreams, live in an expensive home and have three children.
While some of those dreams have come to pass, most of them
have not. Likewise, you probably had ideas of what you wanted
as it relates to career, relationships, finances, friendships and
so on. While those childhood fantasies were cute, maturity dictates that our expectations for those fantasies adjust themselves
to more realistic aspirations and goals.

But what happens when we don't make the shift and those
well-intended ideas are derailed due to unforeseen circumstances like sickness, loss, setbacks, or lack of opportunities?

The answer is simple: we hurt. When our dreams are deferred, we struggle to make sense of our purpose. We settle for what's practical and allow quiet resentment to grow within us until it eats away at our joy and peace. Ultimately, we keep building our world around the hope that these dreams will "one day" come true.

A good friend of mine always dreamed of getting married and having a house full of children. She talked about it often and picked out children's names, had ideas of where she and her future spouse could live, and so on. She prided herself on waiting patiently and staying virtuous to her goals of being abstinent. But her twenties turned into her thirties, and as she moved closer to her forties, she became disillusioned at the reality that she may never get married and have children. Now in her mid-forties, she has given up the idea of having children or possibly getting married—and has grown extremely depressed due to it.

Our greatest struggle in living audaciously is being able to accept the inequity between our reality and dreams. We want our lives to work the way we envisioned. When it doesn't, we suffer. We shut down. We lose hope. We abandon our joy. But here's the greatest danger: when we don't accept the truth of where we are versus where we wanted to be, our courage needed to embrace what's next is sabotaged.

But I Thought...

Things rarely play out the way we expected. Most of us know this, yet we tend to fall apart when life goes off script. We get stuck and feel as if we have no other viable options for moving forward in life. We say to ourselves, "But I thought…things would be different," or, "I never imagined that I would still be single by this point." Unmet expectations often turn into resentment, frustration and depression.

A few years back, a client came to me distraught, as her marriage and family were falling apart. Her first words to me were, "Niki, I never thought my marriage would turn out this way." As a child, her father had left the family when she was young. She watched her mother struggle to raise her and her siblings. She silently determined that her future children were going to have a male presence in their lives. In her mind, not having a father was the main source of her and her family's suffering.

So, as an adult who got pregnant out of wedlock, she did everything she could to keep the father of her child engaged. She even threatened to keep him from seeing his child if they didn't get married. The relationship turned abusive, and eventually restraining orders were put in place for both. In counseling she learned that she had built her life around a fantasy. This fantasy was born out of the pain of growing up poor and feeling unwanted by her father. She made a promise to herself that her children would never experience this pain and decided to write her own script for her life. But what she learned is that when you try to control the script, your dream will turn into a nightmare.

We create stories in our minds of how our dreams and plans will manifest themselves. Some of these stories were crafted out of painful childhoods. We then try to control every aspect of those stories to ensure they play out exactly the way we envisioned them. But when we do, our dreams become a demand versus a desire. They get reclassified as a need instead of a want, which then gets tied to our goals for happiness.

So you tell yourself, "As soon as I get to this stage, I'll be happy," or, "Once I find a good man, things will get better." If you build a sense of happiness on a future goal, you'll become enslaved by it. You will be driven by an internal demand to "hurry up and get there." Taking baby steps will feel like a waste of time to you. There will be a temptation to rush through everything. So long-term dating, extra schooling, training, etc. will be seen as anchors to your dream instead of necessary stepping-stones.

If any of this sounds familiar, don't worry—you're in good company. I spent years chasing a mirage. I skipped over important steps and necessary doors of growth and opportunity just to get to my imaginary utopia. In the meantime, I disregarded the great things God was doing because it didn't match up with the script that I had created. To move forward courageously, you'll need to reconcile the story in your mind with the story in your life, which is ultimately the only story that matters. Why? Because it's a representation of who you are and what's true. It's a result of the steps you took or didn't take to get to where you are. But if you don't like the story you're in, the great news is you can turn the page and discover what God has written about you.

Shifting Expectations

The need to make your life work according to your expectations will always put you at odds with God's greater plan. It will also create a long season of frustration for you. For years I carried a silent resentment because I expected God to fall in line and "get with my program"—but He didn't. I learned that God isn't obligated to make your dreams come to pass. He is not in debt to ensuring that you obtain future happiness or making sure your marriage, job, family or career goes exactly as you envisioned and fantasized it would.

Notice how I am using the words "you" and "your." The only thing God is indebted to are His promises. He swore to Himself that the plans He has for you are not only good but will surely come to pass. Jeremiah 29:11 confirms this: "'For I know the plans I have for you,' declares the LORD, 'plans to prosper you and not to harm you, plans to give you hope and a future.'"

If you're feeling anxious and overwhelmingly frustrated it may be tied to this notion of how you "should be" living. "Should be" living is comparing where you are with where you believe you should be. "By now I should be married with kids." "I should be living in a home and not an apartment." "I should be better in my walk with God." The danger in "should be" living is you could actually be in a great place. But because it's not the place you expected to be, you miss the opportunity to celebrate the season and embrace what God has for you next.

Don't misunderstand what I'm saying—there is nothing wrong with creating a plan. I'm also not suggesting that you should abandon your dreams if they don't come to pass. Holding on to the hope that your aspirations will become a reality is a necessary component of your Christian faith. Allowing yourself to dream is a revelation of your creativity. Having expectations is a good thing. Just don't marry them. Don't fall head over heels in love with your dreams. Your plans can and will change. Your expectations may shift. What you desired in your twenties may no longer fit the landscape of your life in your thirties or forties. Build your faith and expectancy in God alone.

Psalms 62:5 says, "My soul, wait silently for God alone, for my expectation is from Him." Having an expectation in God means you're no longer demanding that your plans come to pass. You're letting go of the resentment you're harboring because things didn't go your way. Instead, you're placing your trust in God's ability to bring His dreams and plans to fruition in your life.

Here's what's exciting: God is not nearly as interested in meeting your expectations as He is in exceeding them. God's ideas and plans are always bigger than ours. Our dreams don't even scratch the surface of what God wants to do and can do for us. When we write our own scripts and marry our plans, we rob ourselves of the abundant riches that God has stored up for us. God already knows our end. He has seen the hills and valleys we will encounter and has created for us exciting futures that will bring glory to His name.

CHAPTER 12
LETTING GO

"Abundance is a process of letting go;
that which is empty can receive."
—Bryant H. McGill

A few years ago, Ebony, one of my mentees, passed away suddenly. She was young, vivacious, healthy and excited about living her passion and dream as a motivational speaker, wife, mother and minister. She left behind several children, a devoted husband and hundreds of people who adored and looked up to her. Her death sent the entire community reeling. Many questioned their own faith as they couldn't understand why God would snatch away such a promising life. I found the grieving process to be difficult as well. It took me months to accept that she was gone, but more so I struggled to let go of the expectations I had concerning her life and healing.

Have you ever been there? Have you experienced a loss so devastating, whether it be from death, a divorce, or a breakup, that you became stuck? Maybe you began something that looked very promising. It seemed as if it was God's will for you, so you plowed full steam ahead into that dream career, ministry, relationship, or business, but it died suddenly. Now you're left to wonder about what it could have been.

Some people soothe themselves by concluding "it must not have been God's will for me." But what if it was? I believe God is omniscient, which means He knows everything. God is not taken by surprise when unexpected events happen to us. There is nothing that has occurred in your life that God didn't already know about, plan or allow. I also don't think He's making it up as He goes along. God does everything with a greater purpose in mind.

So, loss is purposeful. While He doesn't always explain why, He does empower us to move forward. "Brethren, I do not count myself to have apprehended; but one thing I do, forgetting those things which are behind and reaching forward to those things which are ahead, I press toward the goal for the prize of the upward call of God in Christ Jesus" (Philippians 3:13-14).

But what does it mean to move on? We throw around the term "let it go" so easily, but what does letting go even look like? It feels as if God is asking us to forget the past, people or events that's caused us hurt and pain. The word "forgetting," however, doesn't mean not remembering. It means "to neglect, abandon and no longer care for a thing." Sometimes we carry around the pain of what could have been as though we're cradling a baby. We nurse our grief, thereby causing it to grow. We spend time rehearsing what things would have been like "if only..." The danger in this is we can become so focused on what could've been that we fail to see what is. And this is what letting go requires. It's not forgetting. It's embracing what is. It's accepting the reality of what occurred and being willing to walk through the aftereffects.

Letting go also forces us to acknowledge our need for a Savior. Somehow we've bought into the myth that if things are not going as we planned, we have the power to change them. While there are times we should take back control of our lives, we can't control the outcome. We don't have the power to make someone love us or act in a certain way. We certainly can't predict how a situation will turn out. Whenever we try, we are in essence "playing God," which always leads to more stress, hurt and confusion.

Empty Spaces

At some point you'll be challenged to make a destiny decision to let go of something or someone that's no longer tied to your future. But letting go creates empty spaces. Chances are that person or thing you're having a hard time releasing filled a void in your life. I've found the people and things that are the hardest to let go of normally serve the deepest need and take up the most space.

A young woman I counseled a few years back, serves as an example. She came to me because she was dating a married man. While she understood the relationship was morally wrong, she couldn't and didn't want to walk away from it. They had been seeing each other secretly for about four years. He promised that he would leave his wife and needed her to be patient. She said no one had ever treated her better and she believed he was "the one." But she was becoming frustrated and confused about what she should do.

You might be rolling your eyes in disgust, but she is experiencing what I call "the mistress syndrome." It's something we all struggle with when challenged to let go of dysfunctional, toxic relationships. When you drill down on what drives a woman like her, you'll see she has the same basic needs as you: love, validation, significance, security, and acceptance. If in your childhood or adult life you lack any of these, it creates a huge gaping hole. That hole yearns to be filled.

Unfortunately we're not always taught how to look for love in the "right places," so we tend to grab a hold of whatever comes. We will use people, things, work, school, or children just to fill that space. If that doesn't work, drugs, sex, gambling, pornography, addiction and crime will be our temporary fix. Of course, these things are superficial and can't touch on your deepest longings. But it creates a cycle in which you keep going back to get a refill only to be left unsatisfied, which starts the cycle all over again.

The mistress syndrome is centered around the "promise" that this person or thing has the power to fill the holes in your life. You get sucked into the false advertisement that there is nowhere else to go and no one else around to make all your dreams come true. The moment you attempt to walk away, a carrot is held in front of you again, reminding you that this is "the one." So the mistress stays because she's fallen in love with the fantasy of what she has versus accepting the reality of what is. Her reality is she is worth more, but years of repeated trauma, heartbreak, disappointment, denial, and abuse have convinced her that she is not worthy of the effort and appreciation of anyone else. So she discounts her value and puts it up for sale.

We can see this same pattern everywhere: work, friendships, church, addiction, unhealthy behavior and so on. You may not want to hear this, but we've all played the "mistress" at some point in our lives. We held on to and overcommitted ourselves to people and places because of the "promise" and hope that they could define us and mend the broken places within us.

The Story We Live In

I don't believe my client was confused as much as she was afraid. She was afraid of being alone and having to face the one thing she'd been running from—herself. For years she told herself a story about what it meant to be single. Ever since her father left her at a young age, she believed that she wasn't important enough for any man to stay committed. This story crafted her role as the "mistress" in all her relationships. She consistently connected to individuals who lacked commitment and integrity. While deep down she wanted commitment and love, she was stuck in her story with the ending always being the same—rejection, hurt and abandonment.

What's your story? Everyone has one. It's something you tell yourself that hinders you from moving forward. It's a script you've rehearsed to yourself and maybe to others which justifies your dependence on dysfunctional relationships. My story centered around the belief that I lacked true talent and gifting. I felt that in order to be successful I needed to connect to someone who appeared stronger, wiser and more talented than me—even if it meant discounting who I was. My hope was that I would be built up by them. So I remained committed to dysfunctional, controlling relationships that "promised" validation and significance, but in the end only produced more insecurity and disappointment.

When you get stuck in an old story, it consistently reminds you of your past pain and inadequacies, making it difficult to believe you can be better or receive anything greater than what you've experienced. We stay in unhealthy relationships because we believe the lies in the story—that being alone makes us unimportant, unwanted, and unworthy. We overcommit on our jobs, in ministry, and in other places because we think it will finally validate and define who we are.

Confronting Your Fantasies and Fears

To walk away from any of these can feel like death. I know that sounds dramatic, but it's true. It's challenging to disconnect ourselves from something that defines us and fills an empty space. So we remain stuck and hide behind excuses like this one: "I've put so much time into this relationship that it would be crazy for me to leave now." I call this the time excuse. It's the idea that because you've invested so much time into this person or place, you're obligated to stick around to see it through to the end.

Then there is the loyalty excuse: "They've been with me through everything. How can I walk away now?" The one I've heard the most is the God excuse: "I'm just waiting on God to tell me when to move." While there is nothing wrong with waiting on God, sometimes getting to God's plan requires you to take the first step. Whatever justification you are using will only keep you trapped in an inferior version of yourself. It doesn't matter how much time, effort, or commitment you've dedicated to a person or place—God has a better plan and update for your life. But you have to be willing to change your story and gain the courage to confront your fears.

What's keeping you trapped in a place or connected to relationships that don't value or honor who you are? What are the fears that have co-authored your narrative? The fear that kept my story alive was the belief that one day I would be found out. People will finally recognize that I really wasn't "good enough." Deep down I knew I was significant and worth more, but I didn't know how to tap into that truth—until I changed the narrative. The moment I stopped reminding myself of all my failures and faults, I gained the confidence to become who I already was. In that same year, I took a leap of faith and walked away from the very place and people that I thought I needed to survive.

You need audacity to let go. It takes courage to walk away from something or someone you believe is tied to your very existence. But you can do it. You have more resolve than you think. You can do more than you can imagine. How do I know? While you've created a story, God has already appointed one for you too. In that story you were created to live out His purpose and cause His excellence to be seen through your life. You were not designed to be a mistress, a side chick, or a doormat.

Deuteronomy 28:13 says, "And the Lord will make you the head and not the tail; you shall be above only, and not be beneath." In God's story, nothing in your past or present can erase His design for your life. He took all your mistakes, disappointments, hurt, trauma and pain and divinely wove them together so that "all things work together for good." The story you've written always ends the same way after each chapter: disappointment and more pain. But God's story ends in victory. But in order to step into the story God has written, you will have to abandon your own.

Find Your Alignment

Letting go is a process. It doesn't happen overnight. At least it didn't for me. Nor did it happen quickly for my client. It took her a while to acknowledge that she was tired of being "the mistress" in her relationships, work and family. She wanted and desired more. While she didn't want to face the idea of being alone, she realized she would never get what she wanted out of life by putting her value and worth on the discount rack.

Unless you acknowledge who you really are and who you desire to be, the process of letting go will feel insurmountable. You must identify the contradictions in what you say you want and what you actually have. Here's what I mean: We hold on to people and places because we believe in the promise of what they can provide. But ask yourself, "Am I truly getting what I want?" You desire a relationship that provides security, trust and commitment. But do you actually have that? Or do you have the opposite: distrust, insecurity, drama and disappointment?

You may argue that you don't want to be alone. But in the relationship(s) you have now, how alone do you feel? Are you really in love with this person, or have you fallen in love with the fantasy? At times we can become so enamored with who a person could be that we ignore who they are. If you're contemplating leaving your job or changing ministries, ask yourself, "Does this place really align with my core passions? If not, why am I still here?" These questions are challenging but necessary. Listen to that feeling in the pit of your heart telling you that where you are is not right for you.

Keep challenging your fears. Someone once said, "What you are afraid to do is a clear indication of the next thing you need to do." One of the greatest fears in letting go is the belief that your dreams will be deferred—that maybe you will never get to experience having children, getting married, living financially free or stepping into that dream job. You may start to wonder, "If he isn't the one, then who is?" or "If this place isn't my dream, then what do I do now?"

I shared earlier in the chapter that letting go creates an empty space. Right now you may be afraid that when you step into that empty space you won't find a replacement for what you left behind. Well, the truth is, you won't. That's because

God doesn't want to give you back what you left behind. He wants to give you what's waiting in your future.

I know this sounds like jumping off a cliff with no parachute. But letting go with no visible replacement is the ultimate act in audacity. It's a faith sign that you're placing all your dreams, hopes, and desires into God's hands, trusting that He will return them to you according to His will and purpose for your life. I also believe that some empty spaces can only be filled by God. When we run to people and things to take God's place, or to become our source of affirmation and validation in life, we will inevitably be disappointed. But God will use your disappointment in people to develop your faith in Him.

Believe In Better

To be free, you must change the belief system about what you're holding on to. If you imprison yourself to the notion that where you are is "it" and "no one else will ever treat me like this" or "there is nowhere else for me to go," your vision will shrink and your growth will become stagnant. There is always something better waiting for you. God's wisdom, power, and plan are infinite. There is absolutely no limit to what He can do in you and through your life. When we say "this is it" or "there's nothing else," we put God in a box (if that's even possible) and restrict how He can show up in our lives. Often the question is not whether there is more for you, but whether you believe you can have more.

Do you want something better? If you've been stuck in one place or connected to someone for a long time, it's hard to answer that question. You're probably convinced that you have no other options. But search and listen to your soul. Your soul was built for more. When it's out of alignment with its purpose it will ache and become restless. You will have trouble sleeping or doing the things you used to enjoy. You may even realize you're not the person you once were and have no clue how to recover that person. But you can get to better. You still have time to see your dreams and desires come to pass.

You might be reading this and saying, "Well, Niki, you don't know how long I've been waiting. You don't know how many times I tried. I give up. I will just settle for where I am." Here is a truth I had to learn about waiting on God for better. It doesn't have to look the way you envisioned for God to bring your heart's desire to pass. God will often honor the principle of what we want—but He won't always honor the process. Meaning, when your desires align with His will for your life, He will bring those dreams to pass. But He won't do it the way you want Him to—nor when you want Him to. He's not our genie in the bottle. He doesn't work for us as an employee. He is sovereign. Our job is to trust His timing and know that He will bring our dreams to pass right on time. Not one day late and not one day too soon.

CHAPTER 13

GRACE TO SAY GOODBYE

"If you're brave enough to say goodbye, life
will reward you with a new hello."
—*Unknown*

So how do you walk away? Should you completely stop talking to them? Do you block them on social media and refuse their calls? Should you slip your resignation letter under their doors or schedule a face-to-face meeting? These are legitimate questions as one approach doesn't work for all. The concern most people have with ending a relationship is the response they will receive. Too often we allow our hurt, disappointment, confusion and bitterness to guide the process. But this will cause the transition to turn acrimonious. There is a graceful way to exit, and you can find the "good" in "bye" if you realign your heart to what God is doing in your life.

The first step in walking away gracefully is the act of acceptance. It's accepting that the relationship or partnership is over. You've come to the end of a chapter in your life. Acceptance is the fifth and final step in the grief cycle that each person must navigate when experiencing a loss whether it be a relationship, job, divorce or death. Acceptance is the hardest stage in letting go because it requires fully embracing that your reality has changed and something or someone you once loved is gone. Acceptance is also difficult because it reminds us of our finiteness or rather our inability to fully change or fix the things that are out of our control.

The need to be in control of what you can't control will cause you to engage in dysfunctional strategies and patterns to avoid letting go. For example if you don't make a conscious effort to accept that a relationship is over you will find ways to resuscitate it. You may give and do more in the relationship as a way of keeping it alive. Or you might become controlling of that person for fear of them walking away. While this is happening you're silently becoming more angry, resentful and eventually depleted from your efforts of trying to provide life saving measures or what I call "mouth to mouth" resuscitation to a relationship or season that has already died. For some people it takes years to realize that in order to be healthy they will need to move on.

To do this you will need to make peace with the notion that God is involved with this loss. This is important because sometimes we look at the behavior of the individual as the reason for walking away. In other words, you may be walking away simply because they abandoned the relationship first, or you were terminated or let go unexpectedly. This will not only cast blame onto that individual but also tempt you to hang on. Furthermore, you will struggle to gain closure because it wasn't mutual. The same holds true if you are the reason for the separation. You may want to redeem yourself or fix where you messed up.

To walk away you must remove blame. I believe everything works out the way it's supposed to. God is not passively watching our lives and hoping for the best. He is actively working behind the scenes to ensure that His will and purpose are being fulfilled. So whether you initiated the breakup or it was initiated through some other circumstance, you must embrace that God is allowing this season to end and He no longer wants you to hang onto what He is releasing you from.

Look For Capacity

Secondly, accept the idea that some of the people who started at the beginning of your story won't make it to the end. They were never meant to. Those relationships were just the scaffolding you needed to grow during that time in your life. My former pastor had a saying, "Take the meat and leave the bones." This meant accepting the parts of the relationship that were beneficial to you and letting go of the parts that were not. Every relationship has a purpose.

And even if it was dysfunctional, it should have taught you something about yourself. Some of the best lessons I learned about self-acceptance came through the rejection of others. I also didn't know how selfish, self-centered and attention-seeking I was until I had some important relationships end. Look back at the people or places you had to walk away from. What did you discover about yourself? What part did you play in the relationship, and how have you grown from it?

When relationships end abruptly, we tend to demonize the person when in actuality he or she was never meant to continue the journey with us. Or we try to make that person feel guilty about leaving us by weaponizing social media and text messaging to send subliminal messages communicating our disappointment. But these tactics result in more stress and hurt. When someone's purpose has been completed in your life, let them go.

Here is something else that happens which makes letting go difficult—we give people titles and roles they never agreed to and don't have the capacity to fulfill. For example, if you label someone as your "sister," but they haven't been a good "friend," you set yourself up for disappointment when they don't actualize those "sisterly" qualities that you desire. The same thing can apply to our spiritual leaders. Sometimes we've given out titles like "father in the ministry," "mentor" or "intercessor" to individuals who are not qualified for the job. And when the relationship doesn't live out the way we expected, we become angry, bitter and possibly disillusioned with God.

Some people don't have the capacity to be what you need. It's just that simple. They may not have the skills, ability, experience, or knowledge to fulfill the expectations in your life. You may have looked at who they've presented themselves to be and assumed they could meet those needs. Or you thought that because of their relationship to you it automatically meant that person *should* have those skills and ability. For example, one of the common statements I would hear in counseling from clients who were angry at a family member is "but he's my father, he should be there for me." Or "she's my sister and I can't even confide in or trust her. You should be able to trust your own sister." The temptation is to stick around and hope that one day this person will magically change.

But here's a truth I learned while healing from my own disappointments in relationships: you cannot grow a person's capacity to love and give, nor can you will them into becoming the individual you believe or hope they could be. You may have told yourself, "But he/she can change. No one is perfect. We should accept people as they are." You were correct in that people can change. But here's a reality check: you don't have the power to change them. Only God can. And if they are not submitted to God's transforming process, you will be forced to carry them along the way.

Here's another reality check: if you've accepted them as they are, what incentive do they have to become something more? I've often told clients in counseling, "Don't date potential." Don't commit yourself to a person for what they "could be;" you deserve someone who already is.

The same holds true when walking away from a business relationship or place of employment. You might be hoping things will change. Maybe your boss will finally realize how wonderful you are and recognize your efforts. So you've committed to working harder and staying longer. You can be gifted, talented and even have big ideas for your place of employment, but those ideas may never become manifested simply because they weren't meant to.

If you try and make those things fit, you will only become more frustrated and disappointed. Realize that you may have to leave to grow into that professional you envision. Have faith in knowing that if you walk away, you're not abandoning your dream; you're leaving the place that can't contain it.

You may be wondering, "how can I trust the next relationship, ministry or place of employment will not be a disappointment like the others? It seems like I'm on a repeat cycle of getting into relationships that leave me hurt and confused." The answer is one I discovered for myself after walking away from a toxic relationship a few years ago: *look for capacity.*

Before committing to a new relationship, friendship, or place to work or serve ask yourself, "Does this person or place have the ability to meet my needs? Will I be able to grow? Or am I settling for the "potential" of what could happen, or who they could become?" To receive more in your relationships, let go of the notion of who that person "should be" based on their position or title. Discover what makes this new relationship qualified to earn your trust and if the capacity is available for the relationship to be a success.

Critical Conversations and Boundaries

Once you've embraced the fact that it's time to move on, confirm it with a conversation. Some relationships may not require one because the dynamics have changed to where it organically died on its own. In that case, it's time for you to stop grieving and walk away. If it's dead, don't try and resuscitate it. Rather, bury it and move on. But if you're in an active relationship that you need to walk away from, be honest about it.

I'm pretty old school when it comes to handling conflict. I believe it should be done verbally when possible. Of course, if violence or the threat of violence is involved then communicate it in a way that enables your safety. Having difficult conversations is not something most of us relish. It's the reason we often resort to sending an email or text message to communicate our feelings. But sometimes this is ineffective in translating the spirit and energy behind your words, which often leads to misperception and misunderstanding.

Providing verbal closure is not so much for them as it is for you. Being able to speak your truth requires vulnerability and courage. There is a freedom that occurs when you begin to address the discontent that lies within your heart. As you read this you might be thinking, *But they won't understand or agree.* But communicating your truth is not about getting someone to hear or agree with you. It's about you coming into agreement with yourself and God concerning His plan for you and the relationship.

The conversation may sound something like this: "I know we've been through a lot together, and I want to thank you for how you have shown up for me. While I will always be grateful for that, I think given what we are experiencing in our relationship, it's best that we go our separate ways. I harbor no ill feelings as I believe this is God's will for my life. I will continue to pray God's blessing for you." Be honest, clear and direct. If your feelings were hurt and you were disappointed in the relationship, communicate that. Then become intentional about forgiving them so you can move forward.

During breakups and relationship separation people always ask, "Can't we still be friends?" Your interaction with that person afterward should not create ambiguity or confusion. If the relationship is over your actions should reflect that. If you can become friends without the "benefits" that come with dating, then it's no problem. However, most people have trouble creating new boundaries with someone they've had an intimate relationship with. Continuing to stay engaged at the same level as before will only serve to pull you into what's called a "situationship." We often joke about this term, but it's serious and real. It's when you're connected with someone and you're not sure if it's a relationship or not.

The best thing to do is create distance between you and your ex or friend for a period of time. This includes physical distance, but you may also need to change your friend status on social media. If you realize the individual is having a hard time letting go and wants to keep contacting you, you may have to take extra steps to help him or her get the message that you're no longer available. You might need to do the same. If you're struggling with seeing this person move on, unfollow them on social media. Be intentional about creating space and giving your heart time to adjust to this person being absent.

Some of these principles can be used when leaving your place of employment or ministry. Fully disengage yourself from the daily worries that used to consume you. Let go of the idea that you're the "only" one that can do the assignment or job. There are plenty of others who can take your place. And even if they don't, you are not obligated to stay until they do. Release yourself from the burden of being the "savior." There is only one Savior, and He did a pretty awesome job of rescuing us.

It may sound extreme at first but there's no such thing as half walking away. You may even resist some of these suggestions because you're so used to the connection. Don't worry— you and they will heal, and those people will learn to move on without you. If you are consistent in unraveling yourself from dead relationships, you will discover that there is life beyond the grave. The relationships and dreams you have to release will make space for something new to grow and manifest.

You don't have to settle for less than you deserve. Have the audacity to own and value what God put inside of you. You deserve to be loved. You have the right to engage in meaningful, purposeful relationships that challenge you to grow and become better. Allow the flame of God's purpose to grow stronger than your fear of being alone. Just remember God never closes one door without opening a new one.

PART 6
AUDACITY TO LEAP

CHAPTER 14

LESSONS IN LEADERSHIP

*"Become the leader of your life. Lead yourself to where
you want to be. Breathe life back into your ambitions,
your desires, your goals, your relationships."*
—Kevin Cashman

I never wanted to be a leader. To this day I can't pinpoint
when I actually embraced the title. I sort of evolved into
it. I know some individuals have natural leadership instincts.
These instincts probably showed up on the playground when
they were children and took charge of leading their friends to
the swings or deciding what games everyone was going to play.
Then there are those who were somewhat pushed into leadership. I fit into this latter category.

My first leadership experience happened in the fifth grade
when my teacher went on maternity leave. The substitute who
replaced her didn't give us the sense he wanted to be there. He
didn't put forth any effort to connect or teach us the material
the teacher left behind. As preteens, we took full advantage

of his lack of engagement and became absolute terrors in the classroom. One particular day I got pulled into a conversation in which several classmates were complaining about his lack of help and concern. I listened intently and finally said, "We should go to the principal and make a formal complaint." Everyone seemed to like that idea, and for some reason I was nominated as the spokesperson to lead the campaign to oust our substitute teacher.

Emboldened, I promptly marched down to the office of our principal, Mrs. Landrum, and gave her my spiel. I somewhat expected her to dismiss my complaints and politely but firmly send me back to my class. On the contrary, she listened and said, "I'm setting up a meeting with you, the other students and Mr. Branch." I walked away feeling victorious but terrified. Did I really want a meeting to discuss how I felt? How had I become the ringleader for this?

When I told my classmates about the scheduled meeting, they all patted me on the back and we discussed how we were going to "speak our minds" and "tell it like it is" to Mr. Branch. On the day of the meeting, Mr. Branch was in a foul mood—more than usual—and I sensed it had something to do with our meeting. I became very fearful and doubted my decision to speak up for the group. This feeling of doubt only increased once the meeting commenced, and all of my classmates who swore they were going to "tell it" became deathly quiet.

After several minutes, Mrs. Landrum pointed to me and said, "Niki, since you started this...why don't you share what the issues are." Reluctantly I proceeded to tell Mrs. Landrum our complaints. Toward the end of my soliloquy I became more impassioned and requested to have Mr. Branch removed from the classroom. Mrs. Landrum looked amused and dismissed us back to our class. I fully expected Mr. Branch to come back, pack his things and leave. But that never happened. On the contrary, he stayed the entire year and as retribution for the meeting, he made a point to single me out verbally for any infraction I incurred.

I remember going into my shell and deciding to never be a "ringleader" again. I internalized the notion that stepping up to address an issue or fix a problem would only result in more conflict. Of course, I was too young to understand that the way we went about addressing our substitute teacher concerns was inappropriate. I also had failed to exercise any empathy of what it felt like to manage a classroom full of hormonal, out-of-control preteens. Either way, I had no desire to experience the isolation of leadership again.

Leadership By Choice

What I eventually learned, however, is that leadership is a call. Denying your leadership instinct will not make it go away. When you're called to be a leader, it's impossible not to be drawn to people and places that need to be led. Like a moth to a flame, you will find yourself drawn to leadership positions even when you are not seeking them. Suppressing this inclination will only cause you to resort to playing what I call the "reluctant hero" role. You can find this character in almost every action movie, such as the Hunger Games where the heroine, Katniss, only stepped up because she didn't want to see her younger sister play in the Games and possibly die. Throughout the series, she never wanted to lead the revolution but felt forced into that position in order to survive and rescue others trapped by an unfair system.

The answer to the age-old question of whether leaders are born or are made is pretty obvious—you can only become something you already are. I don't believe your purpose, or "call," becomes real when you discover it. Your purpose has always been alive and active—you just may not have recognized it. Whether you were aware of it or not, you have exercised this call throughout your life.

This may explain why you were always designated as "the one" in charge during family events or work-related tasks, or even while volunteering at your church. The leadership title always seemed to find you. Even though leadership is a call, it's also a choice. God will never force you to lead. God gives you the freedom to either embrace being a leader or continue playing the "reluctant hero."

If you resort to the latter, you will miss opportunities to maximize your potential and the possible doors that God wants to open for you. If you exercise the courage to give yourself to it and step to the forefront, God will allow you to accomplish things that you wouldn't be able to accomplish if you had stayed hidden.

The bottom line is this: it takes audacity to lead. Leadership is the ability to motivate and persuade people to engage in a course of action or move toward your desired goal. It takes courage to start a movement. As a leader, you don't always know if your ideas will actually work or if you even have what it takes for people to follow you, which may explain the initial reluctance to lead. In addition, there is a felt burden that comes with increased responsibility. Couple that with the fear of making mistakes as well as dealing with conflict and diverse personalities, and it can tempt the best leaders to hide or pass the responsibility on to someone else.

Lead From Within

While leaders are born, leadership integrity is made. The moment you step to the forefront of a goal, you are a leader. You may not have a full staff of employees, but it's likely you already have a team. The people you surround yourself with from your personal to your professional life make up your team. It doesn't matter how many people are following you or how big your team has become, you will be expected to exhibit leadership behavior, vision, engagement, personality, compassion, patience and courage.

While some of these qualities may come naturally for you, others have to be developed. Over the last couple of decades, leadership and what it takes to be an effective leader have evolved. You need more than just a vision and an ability to supervise others in their tasks. You need to be able to tap into your emotional and psychological profile to gauge what skills need to be developed and matured and which ones will be your greatest assets.

Having a good sense of your own emotional intelligence plays a huge role in your leadership development. Daniel Goleman, a psychologist and science journalist, coined this term "emotional intelligence," or "EI," which is defined as "the ability to recognize and distinguish the difference between your own emotions and those of others, identify them appropriately, and use emotional information to guide healthy thinking and behavior." People who have high emotional intelligence tend to exhibit greater empathy and are self-regulating and self-aware. Studies suggest that leaders with high emotional intelligence lead more effective teams.

What I've learned as a leader is you can only lead from who you are. Leadership is the place where you bring all your gifts, talents, vision, character and heart to create impact and influence. Your team is a direct reflection of this as well as your personality and relational style. Find a team that is personable, energetic and enthusiastic about their vision and you will discover a leader who is compassionate, self-aware, driven, humble and emotionally intelligent. On the same note, if you see a team that is chaotic, disorganized, disgruntled, and non-personable, you will find a leader who is controlling, demanding, narcissistic and lacks emotional intelligence.

Your in-vironment produces your environment. Leadership flows from the inside out. Your values, priorities, personality style, perspective, and psychological makeup will create the culture of your team. Some leaders believe they can create a dichotomy and put on their leader hat at work and take it off at home. While there is some truth to there being a difference in your public and personal persona, good leadership is being able to merge who you are privately and how you show up publicly.

Furthermore, your leadership of others will be dictated by your leadership of yourself. If you don't become the CEO of your own life first, something or somebody else will. In other words, if you have not learned how to manage your emotions, conflict, or responses to certain behavior, you will struggle to lead people effectively.

I've led teams for over fifteen years. I spent the first half of those fifteen years playing the "reluctant hero" and the other half trying to figure out who I was as a leader and what made me distinct. I really didn't have a strong model for leadership and initially just wanted people to help me get the task completed. In my first few years I failed miserably. My teams were disorganized and chaotic. The volunteers were not engaged, nor did they desire to get things done. Many were talking about each other behind their backs, and there was conflict among the leaders and volunteers.

After several years I figured out something important about my leadership—I wanted my teams to accomplish things that I had never addressed within myself. I struggled with being personable, open and empathetic. My emotional intelligence was not developed at a level where I could take criticism or feedback well. I was demanding, controlling and wanted things done my way. This style of leadership dismantled my team and crippled the vision. You can have a great mission, agenda, goal and plan, but if you don't know how to motivate your team to carry the vision it will remain stalled.

My desire to be a better leader caused me to look inward. I decided to stop casting blame and discover what I didn't know about myself that was hindering me from being effective. John Maxwell, Marcus Buckingham and others were pivotal in my leadership growth and maturity, and I learned some valuable lessons on leadership that I want to share with you in this chapter. I call these my leadership lessons.

Lesson #1—Know What You Don't Know

Good leadership begins by finding out what you don't know. Before I could do this, I actually had to admit "I don't know." I didn't know why my teams were having trouble completing basic tasks and following through or what the underlying issues were for the pettiness, passive-aggressiveness, and lack of motivation and energy. I had a suspicion that the results and team dynamics had something to do with my personality and style of leadership. I just didn't understand how.

Admitting that you don't know takes courage. Leaders have a difficult time doing this because they believe that they "should know." A leader fears that if he or she acknowledges that they lack insight, understanding, or adequate skills to address issues or concerns in their team, then others will perceive them as inadequate or unqualified to be in the position. So many leaders remain stuck in operating from what they don't know.

But here's the reality: most employees and mentees are not turned off when you acknowledge a weakness or area that needs growth. In fact, it endears you to them even more. You become less than superhuman. It's very unrealistic to step into leadership and know exactly what to do at all times. Unless you have gone through extensive training or had powerful mentors, your leadership development is trial by error or what I like to call "grow as you go."

Acknowledging what you don't know is also a sign of emotional intelligence because it means you are cultivating a sense of self-awareness. Self-awareness is powerful because once you recognize something, it's impossible to un-recognize it. You have a choice, which is to change or stay the same. Cultivating an awareness of what's driving your internal leadership is key to leadership success.

Self-awareness is like having "the third eye." It's where you step back and take an honest assessment of not only your weaknesses but also your strengths and your wins. We don't spend enough time gauging the tools we've used to create a win. In other words, you're not really certain what you did or didn't do for things to work out the way they did; you're just happy about the end result.

Your level of leadership is determined by the depth of your awareness. As a leader, you must reflect on the steps you took to get to the finish line with a victory and what steps are keeping you in place. Next time you win, stop and ask yourself, "How did I do that?" How do you measure your wins? What is a true win? Is it based on your company's policies and culture? Is it determined by someone else's performance or whether you checked off everything on your to-do list this week? Next time you have a loss, stop and say, "Where was the misstep?" The danger in not knowing what you don't know is that you won't have the insight to excel in your efforts and take your team to the next level.

Self-awareness and discovering what you don't know affects how you impact others and how others impact you. We call this presence (I discussed this in chapter three). While we all have presence, most of us are unaware of the presence that we bring into our teams. To understand the type of presence you carry you need to do what I call an "awareness audit" on yourself by answering the following:

What is the general impression people have of me?

What do people say about me?

What's it like being in relationship with me?

What's it like to be my employee?

Do people feel supported, connected, encouraged, engaged, and heard on my team?

When I show up, does my presence cause people to want to be their best selves?

What frustrates me?

How do I respond when I am frustrated or hurt by those I lead?

How do I reward excellence and hard work?

To answer these questions will require you to become vulnerable. Vulnerability is not a skill set that most leaders like to exercise. The notion that leaders should appear strong, knowledgeable, and well put together goes against the idea of acknowledging our flaws, weaknesses and lack of abilities. So it's easier for some to cast blame and drive the agenda forward for fear of looking like a failure. This will inevitably keep you stuck in what you don't know. But the danger is that you will fail. You will fail to expand your knowledge and leadership skills, and eventually it will prove counterproductive to where you desire to go. Private battles that you don't become aware of will turn into public defeat.

But if you take the risk to discover what you don't know that's contributing to the failure and success of your teams, it will open a doorway for your leadership to thrive.

Lesson #2—Lead from Passion vs. Productivity

We can master the art of leadership but miss the essence. The common emphasis and mantra in contemporary organizations is "focus on people, product, and profits." Many companies have adopted this idea, and the results are evident in terms of high customer satisfaction ratings, great reviews on productivity and increased profits. There are some companies, however, that still drive and reward productivity among employees. In that case, the order turns backward and becomes profits, product and people. The results are also evident in consumer report complaints, low employee engagement scores and high turnover in management.

Talent will become a liability if your passion is only about being productive. Let me share an example. A few years ago, I was working as a leadership trainer for a healthcare organization.

This particular facility was in desperate need of hiring a Director of Nursing who would keep them in compliance. The human resources team hired a nurse who was highly recommended due to her ability to organize, structure and turn difficult non-compliance buildings around in a positive direction.

After several weeks the management team noticed that while she was driven, organized and top-heavy in procedure, she lacked basic soft skills such as communication, conflict resolution, and people engagement. Complaints started to pour in from disgruntled employees. She was accused of "grunting" at people instead of answering their questions. She walked past her nurses every morning without speaking and would tack a list of employees' names who were out of compliance at the time clock. Due to several nurses and CNAs threatening to quit, in less than six months the director was terminated.

What had been impressive about her was no longer important and had now become a liability. Her talent to drive productivity was not as important as ensuring the workers responsible stayed motivated to produce. I call this the Alexander the Great syndrome. He was so driven to conquer the world that he killed the team who would help him conquer it.

Here's another example of this: I was counseling a CEO who was running a nonprofit organization. She was a high-functioning leader with incredible vision, ideas and plans for expansion. The agency was in dire financial trouble, and she was touted as being a turnaround specialist. She developed an amazing strategy to trim down costs and expand services. However, after about a year of employment, she received a significant amount of employee complaints. In counseling, she described her team as a bunch of wimps and crybabies who didn't want to work hard. She felt that it was unfair that she inherited the organization's leadership failures and didn't have time to babysit anyone's feelings.

I've often heard this rationale from leaders when conflicts with their teams arise. They struggle to understand why their teams aren't driven or motivated to produce at the level expected. The idea that people need to come to work, do their jobs and stop whining is a common mantra heard from disengaged leaders. But the results are always the same: employees and volunteers leave because they believe the leaders care more about the product than the people.

Eventually my client was terminated. Even though she was successful in developing a new system and creating a strategic plan for success, her ship was stuck in the harbor. Why? Because the people she needed to man the ship jumped overboard. She won in being transactional but she lost in being transformational. She lost focus of her true passion which was to bring transformation to her community and surrounding regions. She couldn't be successful in this endeavor because she was so focused on getting what she needed that she stepped over who she needed to help her get it.

You cannot get so focused on the goal that you lose sight of the people in between you and the goal. My former pastor used to tell all the associate ministers and pastors that "if you fail with people, you fail." Your greatest passion as a leader must begin with the people. Leadership involves people. Broken people.

Hurt people. Lost people. Motivated and purpose-driven people. Those with high and low skills and some with none at all. As a leader, your duty is to figure out a way to motivate all of these individuals to embrace one common vision, purpose and goal. To do that takes a desire to be a transformational leader—one who inspires change within not only herself but also the people on her team.

I hear you. You're a leader reading this and you're saying, "But the work needs to get done. We have goals and objectives to meet in order to be successful. If we don't produce, we lose revenue, reputation and possibly the ability to move forward." You are correct. You cannot lose sight of the product because you're so involved in managing people. The solution is you must focus on both. I call it having double vision. You have to be passionate about the people and the product at the same time. To do this figure out what's missing for you. Where do you thrive the most and shift your focus to the place that needs to be strengthened.

A powerful way to lead from a place of passion is to remind yourself of your ultimate goal for leading. Why did you choose to become a leader? What are you hoping to accomplish? What changes are you hoping to see within yourself and your team? How can you lead that change? What changes do you need to make within yourself to see this change happen? You may also have to work with a mentor, boss, or coach to learn how to create or enhance a positive culture of engagement.

I'm reminded of the story of Moses when God called him to lead the nation of Israel out of Egypt. Moses wasn't excited about the assignment, and in his discourse with God he said that the people would not believe him or follow him. But God revealed to Moses that the staff he carried would be the tool he used to help the nation become delivered and walk into the promise. The greatest asset you have in your leadership arsenal is the staff that's in your hand. Your team is your best weapon to win and succeed at your goals.

Lesson #3—Abandon the Superwoman Syndrome

I mentioned to you in earlier chapters that I am a perfectionist (in recovery), which means I tend to be controlling, detail-oriented, and slightly demanding when it comes to working toward a goal. This personality style works well for projects that need attention to detail, structure, organization, focus, determination, and drive. People call on me (and individuals such as myself) because they believe I can get the job done or die trying.

This personality style doesn't work well, however, when it's time to collaborate with a team and share responsibilities. Perfectionists have a difficult time letting go of control and allowing others to step into their lane. Furthermore, they live and breathe by the motto "If you want something done, do it yourself."

On the flip side, perfectionists often complain about the lack of help, support, resources, concern or care given by their teams and/or superiors. But when offered help, the perfectionist will often refuse or respond with "No one else has the skills to really do this job." You may not label yourself as a perfectionist (most perfectionists will not), but if the pattern sounds familiar, it's a sign that you may be handicapping your efforts to succeed.

Leaders who believe they have to do it all end up suffering with the superwoman syndrome. This is what it looks like at the leadership level: you micromanage your team, take over duties that you shouldn't, and refuse to delegate assignments to others qualified to handle the job. The superwoman syndrome can cause you to feel guilty that perhaps you've cheated others if you are not "the one" doing it all. Your greatest fear is that you will fail. So you control the people and the process to ensure that success will happen.

The results? A leader who is stressed, overworked, and lacks the time to coach and build others on her team. Working at this pace will prevent you from having the time to cultivate a vision and develop new strategies and goals for your business or organization. You'll be so encumbered with overseeing the daily duties and assignments of your team that you won't have the opportunity to advance. The leader who refuses to let go will fail. As an organization or business continues to grow, evolve, and develop, it needs a leader who knows how to delegate her authority to others who can lead the company more effectively in each area. In other words, it needs a leader who can let go of needing to do it all.

Too often we handicap our help. We keep others from helping when we fail to delegate our power and authority enough. Or when we do, we take it back too soon. You might be saying,

"Niki, when I tried to get people to help me, it ended up back in my lap. Or they didn't do it well." As part of the letting go process, the best leaders learn to empower the people they're bringing alongside them to become the future leaders. This can only happen if leaders are willing to give the new leaders ample control.

Ask yourself: "Do I really trust them to the point that I'll let them make tough decisions? Do I trust them to learn? Do I trust them to grow? Do I trust them to experience their own failures?" This principle doesn't just apply to your leadership team; it should also apply to your life. Have you set yourself up to be the go-to person for everything? Are you overextending yourself to rescue, save, carry and support family and friends when you shouldn't? Are there others to whom you can delegate your responsibilities?

If you've answered yes to any of the above, you're robbing yourself of the opportunity to manifest greatness. You can only increase your capacity to accomplish your dreams by connecting with others who can help you achieve them. As a leader, if you build a culture that empowers the leaders you bring in, it will cause your business to scale and extend its reach. If you trust those around you to help you carry the vision, you will see that vision come to pass.

In your personal life, the same holds true. I can wager that there are fewer people who need to be carried or rescued than you believe. Change the narrative of what you think it will mean if you tell more people no. Embrace the idea that no man or woman is an island of their own. Empower your children, family members and friends to support you in your weekly responsibilities. And if you don't have that large of a tribe, learn how to let some things go unfinished.

As a leader of a team and in life, you are expected to ask for help. I know the "h word" is not very popular among leaders. Asking for help requires courage and vulnerability. I know. I struggled for many years to do it. My pride wouldn't let me acknowledge my inability to be all and do it all. I saw asking for help as a sign that I didn't have it all together. But the truth was I didn't have it "all together" and I wasn't supposed to.

My leadership call was not to go on a solo mission. I was called to lead others to *help* carry the vision and mission that God had placed in my lap. So, after failing miserably at multiple projects and being exhausted to the point of depression, I realized that delegation was my friend. I let go of what I thought others expected to see or receive from me and I embraced this truth: the level to which you achieve greatness will be determined by the level of your support.

Lesson #4—Develop The Right Team

John Maxwell, a nationally known expert in leadership development, said, "The definition of a nightmare is a big dream and a bad team." Have you put the right people on your team to accomplish your vision? Sometimes the barrier to getting incredible results is not the lack of resources but failing to build the right team. You can have a wonderful plan, business idea, and concept, but if you have the wrong people, you will fail to reach a goal you were meant to achieve.

I've coached and counseled leaders who have blamed their teams for the lack of success of the organization. While some of their complaints may be valid, you get to decide who is on your team. As an associate pastor of a large church, I was responsible for overseeing a department with multiple programs and ministries all run by volunteer support. The difficulty in leading these teams was that as a paid employee, my success was dependent on volunteers.

Unfortunately, there is a negative saying about volunteers among leaders: "you get what you pay for." It took me years to learn how to lead and build teams with people who couldn't dedicate as much time as I had but were passionate to serve and grow. I tell leaders, "If you can motivate volunteers to work as if they are being paid, then you can lead anywhere."

There are two important principles I learned about team building that helped my department succeed. The first principle is this: if you pick inexperienced people, you won't get next-level results.

I get it. You're saying, "We need help now. When you need help you can't afford to be choosy." But limited resources + high demand = an atmosphere of desperation. Grabbing anyone who's willing is a gamble and rarely pays off in the end. You will more than likely find yourself complaining that "good help is hard to find" and putting your superwoman cape back on again.

When developing a team, a person's capacity is crucial. The key to choosing a good team is to recruit people based on their supply versus your need. In other words, you have to investigate whether this individual has the capacity to work on the level that you require. Do they have the right skill sets? Do they have the time to invest? Are they available?

I've made the mistake of recruiting individuals who were gifted but didn't have the time or the emotional space in their lives to really put in the work. They were in the middle of a life crisis and had a lot of things going on that prevented them from investing the time. New recruits may not readily tell you they don't have the time. When a person hears about a great opportunity to possibly work in an area of her passion, she will likely not refuse the opportunity. Joining your team may serve as an escape from her issues, or she may be truly unaware of what it will require to meet your expectations.

Sometimes we can get so dazzled about a person's potential that we lose focus on discovering his or her capacity. Capacity is everything. You cannot build an individual's ability to do or be more. Some leaders make the mistake of recruiting people who have great prospects to up-level their skills and knowledge, but they have limited motivation and drive to change. You will never force someone to maximize their strengths and skills. You can only empower them to grow by coaching and mentoring, but if they choose not to embrace it, change will never occur.

Another reason some leaders have a difficult time developing the right team is that they believe that they can do it better. They feel like they know more than others because of their expertise in the business. If you are an entrepreneur and you came up with the idea for the business—and have been at the center of it from inception—it's difficult to bring in other leaders and let go of your control of certain duties.

Some leaders struggle with insecurity and are afraid of bringing anyone more talented and smarter around them. Their silent fear is that they will lose influence, or worse be knocked out of their position. So they inadvertently engage in power struggles to maintain dominance and importance. But in essence when leaders do this, they are handicapping their own help. Other times leaders set the bar so high that even the most talented individuals get frustrated and want to quit. The leaders' rationale is that they want to clone others to be just like them. So they expect and demand perfection. When they don't receive it, they revert to micromanaging and complaining that good help is hard to find.

In his book The 21 Irrefutable Laws of Leadership, John Maxwell discusses the law of magnetism and building your teams, saying that who you attract is not determined by what you want but rather by who you are. Leaders will often attract their strengths. But great leaders will *staff* their weaknesses. Great leaders will recruit people who are better than them. When you recruit someone who can do a better job than you in a particular area, celebrate that. It means your team is being set up for success.

You shouldn't be the smartest person in the room. Your growth and that of the teams are dependent on you aligning yourself with different gifts, skills and talents that help extend your reach. In addition, you may spend less time teaching and training when you bring more experienced individuals on the team.

When you're secure in your ability to lead, you won't feel the need or the pressure to be the "know it all" in the business. Learn to stand next to people who are taller, wiser and stronger than you in certain areas. Be confident that your vision, drive and motivation are what attracted them to you in the first place. High-level achievers are attracted to leaders who are stronger than themselves. When this happens, you will unlock your business and organization to evolve.

The second principle I learned about team building is this: Don't put the right people in the wrong place. More often than not when I have coached and counseled other leaders, I learned that they didn't have a shortage of good help. On the contrary, they had the right people in the wrong place. In our fast-paced world and need to accomplish our goals, we don't spend enough time assessing and evaluating a candidate's strengths and weaknesses to decide if he or she will be the right volunteer, employee or partner.

So we place individuals in positions that may not be aligned with their core skills or passions. When this happens, talented individuals will appear as if they are incompetent. You will train and retrain, motivate, and mentor—all to no avail because the issue isn't connected to talent but to their role.

For example, I learned there is a difference between managers and leaders. Managers maintain a system. Leaders create a system. Leaders influence and motivate people to move toward a common goal. While a leader can be a manager, a manager can't always be a leader. If you don't understand this distinction, you will place individuals in a role to lead, create, influence, make decisions, motivate and encourage when they're more naturally gifted at keeping the order, adhering to structure and following through with what's already established.

On the other hand, if you place a leader in a manager role, they may begin to act outside the boundaries of what you desire them to do. They won't have enough autonomy to be creative and exert influence, nor will they feel free enough to implement new ideas and goals. This leads to frustration, despondency, passive-aggressiveness and lack of motivation.

If you want your team to be productive and thrive, if you want your vision and mission to shift to the next level, invest the time in learning what talent you have around you and figure out where they fit.

You have what it takes to lead with audacity. Courageous leadership is what every employee, volunteer, congregant and partner desires and needs. Step out of your comfort zone, let go of your fear of failure and lead with the next level in mind.

CHAPTER 15

THE ONE DECISION

"All growth is a leap in the dark, a spontaneous
unpremeditated act without benefit of experience."
—Henry Miller

"Ma'am, you're going to have to let go." I looked up from the rock I'd been clinging to for ten minutes during my rappelling adventure in Mexico to see my tour guide standing over me. "To get to the next level of the climb you have to let go and let your body fall." I knew it was true. It would be impossible for me to hold on to the side of that mountain and try and get to the next platform. I would have to do a freefall.

I looked down at the 30-foot drop and got mad that I let my husband talk me into this excursion during what was supposed to be "summer vacation." But I had a decision to make. I could either let them pull me up, which would mean I'd have to leave the group and walk the long way around to rejoin them, or I would have to listen to the tour guide and trust the flimsy rope they called a harness to protect me. Because I hated wasting time, I didn't want to be pulled up to take the long way around. Plus, I couldn't look like a punk in front of the entire group who had already passed me, right? There was no going back—I had to let go. So I closed my eyes, prayed and let myself fall to the ground.

Obviously since I am writing this, I didn't die. Nor did I walk away with any major bruises. But I gained a valuable lesson that day. Sometimes destiny requires you to take a fall. I don't mean a "fall" in terms of a defeat or committing a sin. I'm referring to the fact that you don't always get to carefully step into the next level or check to ensure all your "i's" were dotted and "t's" crossed. I'm also not guaranteeing that everything will go according to plan and that you're ensured a win. There will be moments when you'll have to decide to risk it all. And the only harness or safety net you have is your faith in God's love and His ultimate plan for your life.

This reality keeps people stuck on the sidelines, deciding that maybe this year isn't the best year to take a risk. Or rationalizing they need more resources and support or that they don't have the time. The list of reasons for why you're straddling the fence or clinging to the side of a mountain wall could be valid. But you will never move forward if you don't let yourself freefall.

I know this sounds irresponsible and terrifying. But there's no escaping it. At some point everyone must take a dive on the way to destiny. It's letting go of everything to trust God for anything. You may think what I'm saying is non-biblical, but no one in the Bible was excluded. Noah had to risk looking like a fool to build an ark for 40 years for rain that no one had ever witnessed or experienced.

Abraham had to let go of his family and home to go to a place where he had never been and for a promise he would never fully get to witness. Moses had to literally risk his life to rescue the nation of Israel from Egypt. The list of faith heroes goes on and on. But none of them had a business plan, a blueprint, a strong strategy, or an advisory board to guide them through the journey.

This is the heart of audacity. It's having the courage to make a decision that could cost you everything. Sometimes it's not that dramatic. But it can certainly feel that way—especially if you are making a bold move to do something you have never done before or to be someone that goes against what's expected. Whether it's to become a better leader, walk away from a good-paying job to start a business, or believe in something against all odds, your next season into destiny starts with you.

So what is it? That one step you have to take to leap to your next level or solidify a new door opening? You probably already know the decision you have to make. It's not knowing how that decision will affect your life that has you stalled. Here's the truth: God always provides just enough information to help you make the jump but not enough information for you to know how you will land. That gap, the space of the unknown, is where fear lives. It's the place where you invent bedtime horror stories of how your credit is going to be ruined, how your business is going to fail, how the marriage will fall apart, how you can't live without them and therefore can't walk away, and on and on.

If you are stuck in that gap, don't wait for fear to go away. Instead, invite courage in to speak to your fear. Your courage knows something that fear doesn't. It knows that no matter how bad things appear, God has a greater plan. You may not know how things will end or whether you will succeed. But you do know who planned the end. Here's what God says about your end: Jeremiah 29:11 says, "For I know the thoughts that I think toward you, says the Lord, thoughts of peace and not of evil, to give you a future and a hope."

What do you know about God's promises over your life that will enable you to take the leap and fall? The day I had to sign the contract to host my very first IGNITE conference, I knew that God's plans did not include financial ruin or shame. Even though I was living on food stamps at the time, I had a deep belief that God was on my side and wanted me to succeed. Signing that contract was my freefall. God's hand on my life was the harness.

Going Down to Go Up

The way up is to go down. I know it's a paradox, but to get off of that mountain in Mexico, I had to go down in order to go back up to the next platform. We had been ascending for a while when we hit a cliff, and suddenly we needed to leap off. I already told you I am a perfectionist (in recovery), so I couldn't grasp the concept of this, as it felt out of order. Why couldn't the platforms continue ascending and then descend toward the end? It made more sense. But this sudden drop had me confused. I couldn't anticipate what came next. I didn't have time to prepare myself on what to do. On top of that, I learned that if I didn't go down, I would miss my place in line.

There is nothing more frustrating than being in a season you thought was progressive only to encounter what appears to be a decline or a detour. Our natural tendency is to stop and figure out why the decline is happening. We enlist coaches, speak to our ministers, pray, and read books until we can come up with an answer on how to continue our course. How can we fix it and reclaim our momentum? Is it possible that God doesn't want you to fix it but leap into it?

Here's what I mean: when you resist leaping into what appears to be a setback, you inadvertently slow down the process that God is using to move you forward. What feels like a setback to us is a vehicle to God. If you embrace the declines in your life, God will use them to advance and propel you further. Why? Because setbacks and declines force your faith to develop in a way that it never could have if you hadn't gone through it.

When I was hanging on the side of that mountain, I had to tap into a different level of courage and resolve that I hadn't needed before, nor did I know existed. While I hollered at the top of my lungs all the way down, strangely I felt a jolt of exhilaration and excitement. I received a rush of energy and confidence from just doing it. I'm convinced that this is exactly what your faith needs from time to time—an unexpected, all-of-a-sudden turn in the road, cliff on the hill, to awaken courage, new vision and drive.

Think of your faith as a muscle. If you exercise with the same weights in the same way, you'll hit a plateau. To break the plateau, you must introduce another level of tension. There are moments when your faith grows bored. God has a way of inserting life-altering circumstances, unexpected struggles and detours to stir and activate a new season of courage. So don't resist the decline. Leap into it. Make the decision to do something daring that causes your faith to come alive. It may feel like you're not making progress or that you're going down instead of up, but it's just God repositioning you to advance.

The Cliff-Hanger

You've probably figured out by now that God doesn't like to go in order. Meaning, His process for you won't happen in a perpendicular line, nor does He operate in a way that goes from A-Z. God likes to mix things up. While I'm certain He has a strategy, structure and divine blueprint designed for your life, He is not always willing to share all the details with you. There may be some instructions He gives to you that don't fit with the goals you have. But if you wait for things to align themselves perfectly or for God to download more information that makes sense, you will miss what He has for you.

I think if God were living among us in the flesh, He would love suspense movies. Especially the ones with cliff-hangers written into the story. A good cliff-hanger leaves the audience in suspense, desperately waiting for the next series to arrive. But the problem with cliff-hangers is that they don't resolve the problem in the story. You are left to wonder what will happen next. Will the hero die? Will the other characters be victorious and the villain get what's due? This drives control freaks crazy. We feel stuck when we don't know. We desire resolution to move forward. But when God wants to grow your audacity, He will allow cliff-hangers to be inserted into your story.

I am almost certain God is calling you to leap into something that you don't have all the answers to. You probably feel like you're experiencing your own cliff-hanger, stuck in the space between the end of your last story and the beginning of the next. You've been stalled because you're waiting for God to show you what's next. But I believe faith and courage grow best in the cliff-hanger. It's where God won't answer the question marks in your life. He also won't resolve the problem in the plot like your lack of money, resources, support, or clear direction, and He may not remove your enemies. He will leave you wondering but will challenge you to keep walking.

Can you endure hanging in suspense with no answers or support, knowing it's exactly where God wants you to be? If you plan to leap, you must survive the cliff. But God wants you to do more than survive it—He wants you to embrace it. That involves a willingness to possibly go it alone and not have all the answers or understand the next steps, knowing that God is right there with you.

While I'm convinced that God loves to create a good suspense story, He also likes to insert a surprise ending. One that you never saw coming. You need to know that at the end of this journey you're on, God has a surprise ending waiting for you.

It's something that you could have never guessed, planned, orchestrated or predicted. I think our praise and appreciation are more authentic when we realize that God had an amazing outcome waiting for us the entire time.

Don't Move the Mountain—Climb It

As a motivational speaker, I love topics that energize the crowd, such as "moving mountains," "leaping to your next level" or anything else that gets people stirred up. But while these empowerment messages are meaningful, they skip over the law of process. The law of process implies that to leap, you first have to climb. Meaning, there are some necessary steps and processes that have to take place before you make an audacious jump.

The mistake most dreamers make is they see the vision, get excited, take action, and expect immediate results. When the results they were hoping for don't come, discouragement sets in. They lose confidence and put the dream on the back shelf with the distant promise to pick it up "one day when I'm ready." Of course, that day never comes, and they move on to another idea or dream only to repeat the same steps and experience followed by the same results.

When God gives you a dream, He only shows you the end. You have to go back and create the beginning. When I worked as an associate pastor a few years ago, I attempted to establish "family night" in my church. I had this idea of hosting a conference where every member of the family came and engaged in some workshop or activity. In my vision I saw hundreds of people attending, with families loving and laughing with each other. Because I was excited, I ran full steam ahead into planning mode.

However, I didn't take into account that my former church had never experienced anything like this, nor did I understand how to really communicate what I wanted it to look like. I didn't have a clue as to how many partners and stakeholders I would need to engage to make this happen. I never sat down to plan a budget or think through the logistics of what it would mean to have every member of the family show up on one night. Should we have babysitting? Who would entertain the kids? What about the teens and the elderly? Have I considered that it would take place in the evening and the elderly may not want to come? If I would be having classes for men and women, where would the couples go? I didn't have the answers to any of these questions but jumped headfirst into planning the event.

The results were disastrous. The turnout was poor. Most of the leaders didn't understand what I was doing or the role they needed to play. The workshops were not well attended and the food was dismal. I went home discouraged and threw away the idea. I decided that I wasn't going to risk looking like a fool again.

Eventually I realized the problem was not my idea. My problem was the lack of process. I had skipped over important steps that would have made the event more impactful. For instance, I never considered scaling down the event. Nor did I think about the possibility of this being a yearly experience that I could build upon. I wanted to leap over the process and experience the promise. I didn't want to sit in the waiting room in order to see the accomplishment of the idea. I wanted to reap the reward for my courage immediately. My need to get to the end result prevented me from cultivating a good beginning.

For some people the struggle to live audaciously is not due to a lack of faith or courage but a lack of perseverance. We want that "speak to the mountain and it will move" result. But not every mountain was meant to be spoken to. Some mountains you have to climb. In other words, there are some blessings, ideas, dreams and seasons you have to grow into. If you are an entrepreneur, it may mean implementing one part of your dream at a time. If you are in a relationship with someone you think is "the one," it means slowing down before you rush into marriage.

I'm convinced that it takes more courage to climb a mountain than it does to speak to it. It takes more faith to wait for something to manifest than to believe and receive it immediately. You need audacity to carry and nurture a dream from infancy to maturity, especially when you are short on resources and support, and when progress is slow. But there are things you learn in the climb that you wouldn't learn if success came overnight. When you jump too soon, you limit your growth. You shrink your capacity to develop long-term vision and achievement. You handicap yourself in being able to identify your weak spots and the areas where you thrive.

What mountain is God calling you to conquer? What dreams, ideas or areas in your life have you given up on that needed cultivating instead? Find your courage and climb. The promises you're waiting to see are not always discovered in the jump—but are found in the journey.

CHAPTER 16

ANSWER THE CALL

*"You have everything you need to
answer the call of your soul."*
—Marie Forleo

I hope by now you realize that living audaciously means pushing past the outer limits of your life in every aspect: faith, identity, vision, dreams, leadership, and drive. Sometimes that push requires you to fight. But isn't that the very essence of courage? Courage isn't courage if there is no fight involved. You don't need courage for a fight you have the strength to win.

You need courage when the odds are stacked against you. You need it to fight through doubt, frustration, fear, depression, lack of support, validation and overwhelming circumstances. Courage kicks in when you get knocked down...not once but over and over, and God invites you to get back up to fight again.

When Courage Knocks, Answer

A few years ago I wrote my first book, There is More, and I was super excited. But once I started to go through the publishing process, self-doubt crept in and told me that I didn't have a lot of support or venues to which I could sell the book. I pushed through and had an amazing book launch with several hundred women in attendance. Subsequent book sales, however, were not great and I couldn't go on tour the way I envisioned. Feeling defeated, I put off writing another book for several years. If I had it my way, I probably would have never picked up my computer to write again, but God kept tugging at my heart.

God's sense of humor was in asking me to write about courage at a time when I would rather run and hide. But this is courage at its best. It knocks on the door of your insecurity and fear and enters the cave of procrastination where you are hiding and challenges you to come out. If you're waiting to feel very courageous before making a move, you might be stuck indefinitely.

Technically courage is a feeling, but I think courage is also a calling. It's an inner instinct of hope and boldness that shows up in your darkest season and speaks opposite of the fears you held and believed. Answering the call of courage means taking a step and making a decision. I truly believe that a decision is the one thing standing between you and destiny. How do I know? Because you've been fighting to do it. And anything that comes with a fight has a greater purpose attached to it.

So, what door is audacity knocking on? What is courage calling you to do? What mountain have you been challenged to climb, conquer or move? Don't allow fear to steal your inheritance or the ability to enter the next best version of who God has created you to be. You may not have all the tools at your disposal to leap the way you envisioned, but courage will become your springboard. It will advance you in a way that you hadn't thought possible. But not if you ignore its call. You have to say yes first, and then the rest will follow.

And for those who need one more sign, here it is: this book is your last sign. It's what God's been speaking to you all along. If God hasn't been speaking to you it's only because He hasn't changed His mind about what He's already said.

Look Before You Leap

A few years ago while my husband and I were vacationing in the Grand Cayman, we decided to try a watersport called Snuba. If you haven't already figured it out, we are both adrenaline junkies and love adventure. In public I like to blame Harold for pushing me into doing these zany adventures, but secretly I love it. Anyway, Snuba is a cross between snorkeling and scuba diving. The difference is you are attached to an oxygen tank and hose that is sitting in a life raft above water.

The group leader had all of us practice breathing in shallow water before we ventured out into the deep ocean. I caught on pretty quickly and waited for everyone else to finish practicing. While I was waiting, I started to giggle silently at a few of the participants who were "freaking out" and afraid during practice. I leaned over to my husband and whispered, "There is always one or two in the group, right?" Feeling overly confident and a little cocky that I had mastered the technique, I told the instructor I was ready.

Right before we started swimming, the instructor reminded us that we were going down pretty deep and if we got into trouble, we shouldn't race to the surface because the water pressure could damage our lungs. I partially ignored his warning and started swimming. I wasn't far into the descent when I started to feel uncomfortable. My googles were filling up with water, and I was having trouble breathing. After several seconds of trying to see and breathe I gave the sign that I was not okay and started to panic. Immediately I tried to race to the surface, forgetting the instructor's warning about the water pressure.

When I reached the surface I sank several times, as we had a weight belt on us. That sent me into more of a panic so that by the time my husband and the instructor reached me, I was hysterical. My husband and the instructor were not exhibiting the concern or panic that I thought they should—possibly because I had been so cavalier a few minutes earlier about learning a new technique. Once I stopped crying and coughing, the instructor polity informed me that I was holding up the group and needed to decide if I wanted to go back to land, continue with the group, or follow the group by swimming on top of the water which was more shallow.

Before I could answer he quickly disappeared and went back to the group. I think he was sick of dealing with my drama.

I knew my husband really wanted to go with the group, and being a good wife I said, "You don't have to stay with me if you don't want to." I half expected him to play dutiful husband and stay, but my husband didn't let me finish before he said, "Thanks, you're the best" and disappeared back underwater.

As I swam alone and watched everyone go to a depth I couldn't reach, I realized I had become "that one" in the group that I had joked about earlier. I tried to figure out how things failed so quickly. I had to eventually acknowledge that while I was ready to leap, I wasn't ready to handle the pressure that came with what I was leaping into. I had no previous experience in deep-sea diving. In fact, I had just learned to swim a few years earlier.

Swimming in eight feet of water was nothing compared to swimming in twenty feet and going to a depth that I had never experienced before. I made the mistake of believing that one environment was the same as the other and that the same skills I needed to swim in shallower water would help me out in the deep. That led me to misjudge my confidence as courage when it was really cockiness, lacking insight and wisdom.

There are times when you can get so used to swimming in shallow waters that when it's time to launch or leap out into the deep, you become too fearful or gain a false sense of confidence that hinders you from truly navigating your way through new territory. It would be irresponsible for me to empower you to leap if I didn't address the pressure and new challenges that go along with what you leap into. You may be considering going after that director's position this year. Maybe you are fired up to launch your new business idea. All these things are amazing. But are you ready for the burden that is attached to the blessing?

Every promotion has another level of testing and stress you must embrace. The movies and social media make promotion look so glamourous. But we don't see what happens behind the scenes: the late nights, long meetings, stress and pressure to perform or live up to people's expectations. I have met, counseled and coached more people who had the courage to leap but didn't have the maturity to maintain any momentum. They didn't understand what was waiting on the other side, nor did they investigate. They had faith but didn't have a formula for how to create success after the leap.

At times we isolate our faith and make it so spiritual that we neglect the practical. The Bible says in James that "faith by itself, if it does not have works, is dead." Faith requires that you do some homework on where you're going. If you have the faith and courage to do something bold but you don't have wisdom on what comes next, you will fail in something you were meant to succeed in.

In the book of Numbers chapter 13, God told Moses to send men to spy and gather information about the land of Canaan, which God had promised to give to them. Moses chose twelve men and told them what to look for: "Go up this way into the South, and go up to the mountains, and see what the land is like: whether the people who dwell in it are strong or weak, few or many; whether the land they dwell in is good or bad; whether the cities they inhabit are like camps or strongholds;

whether the land is rich or poor; and whether there are forests there or not. Be of good courage."

The question has to be asked, "Why did they need to investigate the land when God previously declared it was a "land flowing with milk and honey?" Why did they need to go through the extra investigation? They could have just said, "God already told us His will, so let's cross the Jordan and take the land!" In fact, that's exactly what happened in Numbers 14 when God told the people they were not ready and would have to wait another 40 years to go to Canaan due to their doubt.

The nation decided they would try and exercise their faith. But they failed because they didn't develop a strategy. That was the sole purpose for sending the spies in the first place. It would give the nation a chance to create a game plan as to *how* they needed to fight, rebuild, grow an economy, and plant crops. Having faith alone for a promise will not guarantee you possessing it. You need a strategy to connect with your faith to achieve the success you were meant to experience. I want to give you some next step strategies to prepare you to leap to your next level:

Get ready to sacrifice

Jesus told His disciples in Luke 9:62, "No one who puts a hand to the plow and looks back is fit for service in the kingdom of God." Jesus was talking to an agricultural society who understood this metaphor. He had been speaking with the disciples about the costs of answering the call to follow Christ. In order to follow Him, one would have to be willing to let go of the former things keeping them tied to the past.

I think we can relate this same principle when making a decision to leap into something daring. As I discussed in Chapter 15, to leap you have to let go. This letting go requires a sacrifice, such as releasing former relationships, expectations, positions or dreams. You may have to sacrifice free time or increase your prayer and fasting regime.

I don't want to imply that you have to work to earn the anointing or God's blessing on your life. None of us can earn God's favor, nor do we deserve it. Salvation doesn't come through works but by faith and God's grace. So too is His blessings in our lives. His grace working through you is what opens the door for you to accomplish audacious things. But your sacrifice is what puts you in a position to receive it.

Discover your blind spot

If you've been driving for some time, you know that blind spots can cause some of the worst accidents. A blind spot prevents you from seeing something that is present but is obstructed from your view. The general rule when switching lanes is that you must look in your blind spot first before turning. I think we can use this same concept when leaping into a new place. Ask yourself the question, what is it about this venture that I don't know or have information about?

Sometimes we can become so dazzled by the excitement and exhilaration of walking through a new door or into a new opportunity that we fail to look for blind spots. This prevents us from navigating the turn correctly. I believe that when Moses sent the 12 spies to the land of Canaan, he was trying to help them find the blind spots connected to the promise. Every promise has a blind spot—something that you can't see concerning where God is taking you. While God may hide some of the details, it's your responsibility to analyze the information that is not hidden.

So before you leap, take a good look at where you are going. What information are you missing? What do you need to see in order to thrive in this new environment? When God told us to leave everything and everyone behind to move to Kentucky, we were excited but nervous. We had never been so far away from home or in a culture that was so different from our own. For me personally, the move was daunting. I was leaving not only a church where I had served as an associate pastor for over ten years but also ministry teams, family and friends.

We knew God was telling us to take this leap, but there were things we didn't know and understand about where we were headed. Were the people nice? Was the city diverse? Would there be any opportunities for female ministers to serve in the local church? How close would we be to entertainment and food? What type of community groups were tied to our passions? Thankfully we were given time to spy out the land. The answers helped to prepare us to develop a game plan for starting over again and devise a strategy to navigate this new terrain.

Build your capacity for more

You can prepare as much as you like but there is an element to the next level that you won't be able to plan for until you get there. What you can do is take an inventory of your life and decide if you have room for more. You may want more, have prayed for more, but do you have the capacity to embrace everything that more brings? You can't predict everything that is going to happen, but you can begin to audit your time and space.

To leap to the next level, you will need to disengage yourself from things and assignments that are robbing you of your time and energy to do more in your life. Take an assessment of what you are doing right now. Identify those things that are not connected to your core passion and mission. Pay close attention to those areas that used to be a key passion but are now an obligation. If you carry your obligations into your next season, you will miss new opportunities to prosper.

Be courageous enough to turn in your resignation or reassign these assignments to someone else. What will be your focus once you leap into the next season? Gain the clarity you need about your mission. Who or what needs more of your time, creativity and energy? Create space you need to grow into this next season. If you don't, someone else will dictate how much space you are entitled to.

Create momentum

How often have you seen an announcement from someone on social media about that person receiving an exciting new job, relationship, or opportunity only to see six months later he or she quit, walked away or experienced failure? I'm not trying to shame anyone, but you have to wonder, what happened? The few people I know who experienced these types of results were not fly-by-night entrepreneurs or individuals who took risks lightly. After speaking with several of them, I discovered the answers to be the same: lack of momentum. They all made bold moves, but once the excitement and adrenaline wore off, they struggled to sustain or even grow the movement.

When IGNITE hit its second year, it was like an explosion went off. So many women came from surrounding cities and towns that we sold out a month before the actual event. I was riding on cloud nine. I had taken that initial leap of faith to start a women's organization and conference and it felt like my faith was being rewarded. I wanted to keep the energy alive, so I took another leap and added a second day for the next year.

I was confident that we would grow our numbers and see even more women. The closer we got to launching the event, we realized that our registration numbers were low—so much so that I realized we would not meet our budget. In addition, because we had contracted at a larger space, we had to scramble to adjust our meeting room to accommodate the number of people attending. I felt so defeated. I vowed that I would not do the conference again.

Despite the low numbers, the conference was amazing. The women who did attend gave great testimonials on their experience. After praying and having several of my good sister-friends talk me off the "ledge of quitting," I decided to do it again. But first I had to understand what happened.

My first mistake was not understanding my audience and their financial limitations. The conference generates more of a church crowd with women who are not used to paying a high registration ticket. Secondly, I assumed that because women enjoyed the one day that they would immediately embrace taking off work the next year to come for two days. I also didn't factor in the logistics of changing the location and how people would react to this change.

While I knew how to put on a great event, I didn't have the knowledge to scale and create sustainable growth. So before you leap, strategize what will happen afterward. How will you maintain the momentum? What steps will you take to sustain the energy that your efforts bring while creating growth in incremental ways?

Here are a few key steps that I used to create some momentum in IGNITE after that challenging year, which you can use for your business, ministry and life:

Think Big—Start Small

Some people reject the idea of starting small because it goes against their larger vision. But starting small doesn't mean "thinking small." Your beginning starts with baby steps. Think about it in terms of driving your car. When you step on the gas, your car doesn't immediately accelerate to 75mph. You have to gradually increase your speed as you go. The same is true for anything new you begin: exercising, losing weight, writing a book. Even God had to start small. Genesis recounts how God systematically created the world in seven days. He could have finished it in one. But God obeyed the principle of momentum. Everything starts small.

To grow IGNITE I had to scale back the vision and create implementation phases and goals. I decided to implement one new idea each year instead of doing them all at once. I also looked to see how I could strengthen my core foundation for the summit, which included restructuring my core team, evaluating our effectiveness through surveys and consistency, and reassessing my brand and overall mission.

Think about what you want to accomplish. Take out a piece of paper and jot down all your ideas. From that list put a star next to the top three goals that you would like to accomplish first. Create a realistic timeline to accomplishing this first set of goals. Then do the next three, and so on. Use the accomplishment of these goals as a starting point to accelerate into the next phase of goals. Eventually you will gain momentum and discover that big things indeed come from small beginnings.

Be Consistent

Dreamers and entrepreneurs tend to be burdened with new ideas every week. Literally. I should know—I live with a dreamer. These types of people feel pressured to hurry up and implement their ideas before someone else beats them to it. So before they finish one idea, they are leaping to the next, and when they get another inspiration, they leap to that one...and so on. It gives most of them the appearance of being flighty and unbalanced.

If you are a dreamer or entrepreneur and you are reading this, you are not alone. But here's a truth: you can be gifted and creative with million-dollar ideas, but if you never build momentum on any of them, it's pointless. Entrepreneurs must embrace the art of discipline and process in order to thrive. So I use the same exercise above to help them get laser-sharp clarity on which idea they need to begin. Inconsistency is a habit—one that needs to be broken if you are going to see any momentum. Decide on the one or two goals you need to work on to move the needle forward in your business, profession, ministry or life. Give yourself a 30-day challenge to consistently work on it.

I knew that if I was going to finish this book I had to structure my day around an intentional goal of being consistent. Especially since I don't like to write. I couldn't build momentum by working on the book every now and then or when I felt inspired. I had to literally schedule time every day to write. No matter what. It won't be easy, especially if you are a thinker and have a constant barrage of new ideas, thoughts and tasks that are vying for attention.

I had to do the same thing when planning IGNITE. I know that my weakness is procrastination. I also know that my team feeds off of my energy. If I am inconsistent in meeting deadlines or goals and procrastinate on projects, I will only recreate that same pattern among those who follow me. I challenged myself by creating a consistent planning guide that helped me to stay on track with our mission. Consistency creates acceleration and movement. Being diligent takes patience and practice but yields sustainable results. If God gave you the ideas, I am a firm believer He is going to grace you with the ability to implement them.

Break Boundaries

You will never build momentum if you're content with being safe. This sounds funny for me to write because I have always shied away from taking big risks. It's probably why God had me write this book. What I do understand is that you will never accelerate if you maintain. A few years ago, my husband and I were teaching our daughter, Myka, how to drive. If you have kids in this age range, you understand how harrowing this experience can be. What I didn't realize was how nervous she would be either. So for several weeks we had her driving in the neighborhood and in parking lots. But eventually we knew that if she was really going to learn and grow, she would need to hit the highway.

When we got on the highway, we had to explain that as safe as it felt to continue driving at a comfortable speed, she would need to increase it significantly. This made her nervous, as she thought that she was breaking the speed limit. But throughout the journey we kept encouraging her to "increase the speed" until she accelerated enough to merge with the oncoming traffic. At some point in your life you will need to break your own speed limit. To create momentum, the rules and boundaries which kept you at a certain pace will have to be broken and adjusted to fit a new set of goals. Accomplishing new goals and dreams will require you to do something you've never done before and stretch yourself outside your comfort zone.

This year God impressed upon my heart to change the venue of IGNITE. I had grown very comfortable in the facility we'd been using for the past three years. But it was clear to everyone that we'd outgrown it. I looked for comparable facilities in the area that could house our growing numbers but came up empty. The more I prayed about it, the more I felt that God was asking me to take another leap. I contacted a convention center in Delaware, and after much prayer we took the jump to host our conference in a place larger than our current crowd and budget size. What I am coming to understand is that to stay relevant in a culture that is always changing, I couldn't maintain the same pace that brought me success five years ago. I needed to "increase my speed."

Sometimes breaking barriers simply means doing more in an area you're already in to break a plateau and achieve a greater outcome. A great example of this occurs in exercising. A few years back I wanted to lose some weight and did everything I could to no avail. After speaking with a trainer, I learned that I had hit a plateau. Because I was already working out, my body had adjusted itself to my routine. So no matter how healthy I ate or how intense my exercise regimen was, I wasn't going to lose any more weight. I needed to increase the frequency and introduce tension by weight training. After a few weeks I started to see dramatic results in my weight loss. I learned that tension was my friend.

Don't shy away from assignments or opportunities that are designed to stretch you. While it takes courage to break any barrier or pattern that's brought you success in the past, if you've gotten this far in the book, you're ready to be audacious enough to throw caution to the wind and give your life the opportunity to soar.

CHAPTER 17

YOUR TIME IS NOW

"So many of our dreams at first seem impossible,
then they seem improbable, and then, when we
summon the will, they soon become inevitable."
—*Christopher Reeve*

A re you ready? No, are you really ready—to leap? I'm a firm believer that there's an entire world waiting to receive what's inside of you. Your gifting and calling are unique. No one can duplicate it. It has to be fulfilled by you. But I get it. You've had some difficult circumstances to face, overwhelming mountains to climb and impossible odds to fight through.

On top of that, you believe time is slipping away and the things you desired to do feel ancient. Maybe it's too late. You're saying, "I really want to take that next step. I want to leap, but where am I going to find the strength, let alone time, to do it?" My argument back is simply this: time and strength are not hiding from you. You don't need to find it. You simply have to receive it.

Hebrews 11:11 says, "By faith Sarah herself also received strength to conceive seed and she bore a child when she was past the age, because she judged Him faithful who had promised." Sarah was ninety years old when she finally gave birth to a son. At some point Sarah believed in God's faithfulness to do exactly what He promised her and Abraham. It was her faith and courage in the face of insurmountable odds that God honored and caused Him to release the strength she needed to give birth.

It doesn't matter how old you are, the length of time you've had to wait, or all of the circumstances you've experienced—God wants to give you strength to conceive and leap into your destiny. Courage is the incubator God uses to renew your strength and passion. If you show God your courage and faith, He will reveal your ability to step into the impossible.

I want to make another bold claim. The barriers you've been facing are intentional. I have a suspicion that your obstacles are opportunities to test what you have learned concerning God's faithfulness and love toward you. Look back over your life, especially at the times when you were not aware of God's presence. You will see He was there. He was leading and protecting you through every circumstance you encountered whether good or bad. I would even say those moments you overcame were preparing you for such a time as this.

This is your moment to prove to the world that God is with you and He is for you. What better way to show off God's glory than to take an audacious leap of faith into the unknown and reveal His power through you? I think it bears repeating that you probably don't need another sermon or sign. If you take the next step, I believe God will make every resource in heaven available to you as a sign that "with God nothing is impossible."

But it starts with you. God will never force you to step out of your box, nor will He condemn you for staying in it. But God is inviting you to experience a version of yourself that you haven't seen yet. You've already done what you think you could do. Now it's time to accomplish what you thought you couldn't do. I dare you to take the challenge and leap. When you do you will discover a whole new world that's been waiting for your audacity to arise.

Listen, you were born to thrive. Your heart and soul were built with a gift that is unique to your DNA. Your DNA is absolutely distinct. That means your talent will never look like anyone else's and what you are purposed to accomplish can never be duplicated.

It will take courage, boldness, tenacity and plain old grit to authentically walk in your uniqueness. And at some point you will come to a crossroads with a choice to make a destiny decision, and you will need the audacity to do it.

Notes

Introduction

1. Brown, B. (2015). *Daring Greatly: How the Courage to Be Vulnerable Transforms the Way We Live, Love, Parent, and Lead.* New York, New York: Avery; Reprint.

Chapter 1

1. Dingman, D.J. (1988). *The Impostor Phenomenon and Social Mobility: You Can't Go Home Again.* Dissertation Abstracts International, 49.2375B.

2. Ravindran, S. "Feeling Like A Fraud: The Impostor Phenomenon in Science Writing." *The Open Notebook,* November, 15, 2016, www.theopennotebook.com/2016/11/15/feeling-like-a-fraud-the-impostor-phenomenon-in-science-writing/.

3. Litner, J. PHD, LMFT, CST. "How to handle impostor syndrome." *Medical News Today,* September 29, 2016, www.medicalnewstoday.com/articles/321730.

Chapter 4

1. Perry, T. (2017). *Higher is Waiting.* New York: Spiegel & Grau/Random House.

Chapter 8

1. Lubbocks, J. (1834-19-13). *The Beauties of Nature and the Wonders of the World We Live In.* New York, Macmillan.

Chapter 10

1. Gans, J. (2016). *The Disruption Dilemma.* Cambridge, Massachusetts: The MIT Press.

Chapter 14

1. Dollard, C. "Emotional Intelligence Is Key to Successful Leadership." *The Gottman Institute, 2022,* www.gottman.com/ blog/emotional-intelligence-key-successful-leadership/
2. Cole, M. "Recruiting the Most Important Member of the Team" *John C. Maxwell,* January, 25, 2019, https://www. johnmaxwell.com/blog/category/hiring-and-firing/
3. Maxwell, J. (1998). *21 Irrefutable Laws of Leadership.* Nashville, Tennessee: Thomas Nelson, Inc.

Made in the USA
Las Vegas, NV
02 May 2022

48346646R00116